When Se.

Although, traditionally, professiona
credibility and legitimacy for a pr
you to hear how other "regular" women in your situation have benefited from this material. Only their first names are being used in respect for their family's privacy.

"When I learned that my husband had been hiding a secret sexual addiction, a rush of emotions and questions began to haunt me. Hurt and angry, and yet wanting comfort and reassurance from the husband who rejected me, I often thought I was going crazy. This book answered so many questions for me, and more importantly, helped me realize that what I was feeling was normal. There were no 'pat' answers - just honest insights into what had happened to my husband and what I could expect to be thinking and feeling myself. This book provides a valuable resource for anyone trying to recover from the devastation of shattered trust."

—**Karen,** *wife of a sex addict*

"For me, finding out that my husband was looking at porn and going to 'dirty book stores' was completely outside my universe. The very thought of his behaviors made me so sick to my stomach that I actually began to lose weight. We didn't talk about it. In fact, I could hardly even stand to look at this man who had been my husband for over 40 years.

I didn't know anything about sexual addiction when I came across Janet's book, *When Sex Causes Heartbreak*. I wasn't even sure I *wanted* to know about it, but reading the book opened my eyes to begin to see and understand my husband's pain. It helped *me* heal. It can do the same for you."

—**Linda,** *wife of a sex addict*

"The pain of betrayal cuts deep in anyone's heart, but I'm not sure that anything cuts quite as deep as sexual betrayal. In the midst of this confusion and hurt, *When Sex Causes Heartbreak* reaches out with a warmth of understanding and a depth of knowledge that helps to start the healing process. It provides a level of assurance that every grieving woman needs. But overall, it is a book that can be turned to again and again throughout the journey toward a deeper intimacy and renewed hope within your own marriage. With insights backed by both biblical truths and years of counseling experience, I highly recommend it!"

—**Natalie,** *wife of a sex addict*

"*When Sex Causes Heartbreak* is a book that *every* woman should read. Whether you have a healthy marriage or a marriage that has you wondering what went wrong, this book provides knowledge and truth about a problem that statistics show is very likely to impact you or someone close to you.

Janet Wheeler has boldly written about sexual addiction and how the actions and thoughts of an addicted spouse can deeply affect you and your emotional well-being.

Within its question and answer format I found, for the first time, many of the same questions I had been asking myself, along with answers that have helped me put aside 'false truths' and move on toward becoming more emotionally healthy."

—**Jane S.,** *wife of a sexual addict*

"*When Sex Causes Heartbreak* is a tool that God used to strengthen my life, my marriage, and my heart:

It gave me an understanding of not only my husband, but also myself.

It freed me from the lies of the enemy and taught me how to apply God's truth to my situation.

It provided me with the insight into my husband's heart that I so desperately needed.

It allowed me to grieve what I had lost within my marriage but also allowed me to cling to the hope that still remained there.

May this book be a beacon of light along the path God has before *you,* as well."

—**Nicole S.,** *wife of a sexual addict*

When Sex Causes Heartbreak

What Every Wife Should Know About Affairs, Pornography & the Sexless Marriage

Janet K. Wheeler

Janet K. Wheeler

All scripture quotations, unless otherwise indicated, are taken from the Holy Bible, New International Version®, NIV®. Copyright ©1973, 1978, 1984, 2011 by Biblica, Inc.™ Used by permission of Zondervan. All rights reserved worldwide. www.zondervan.com The "NIV" and "New International Version" are trademarks registered in the United States Patent and Trademark Office by Biblica, Inc.™

WHEN SEX CAUSES HEARTBREAK
Copyright © 2013 by Janet K. Wheeler
Published by Bluewins Publishing
Bellingham, Washington 98225

Based on a booklet of the same name ©2003 by Janet K. Wheeler

All rights reserved. No portion of this book may be reproduced in any form without the written permission of the author.
ISBN-13: 978-0615874319
ISBN-10: 0615874312

Dedicated to every woman
who walks this lonely and difficult road
with their husband.

Your courage, sacrifice,
patience, and love
have not gone unnoticed.

A Word About Our True Identity

God, in His grace, looks through our struggles and sees the victorious and gifted person we were intended to be. He looks beyond our failures and sees our heart. We must, therefore, be cognizant of the emotional and spiritual ramifications of defining someone by their struggle alone.

When a person is addicted to destructive compulsive behaviors, however, the never-ending cycle of addiction usurps God's place in their life. Even though they may, on one level, love God, the addiction becomes their protector, their guide, and, in a sense, their best friend—all the things that God desires to be in our life. As this happens, the person's true identity is increasingly replaced by an addictive survival personality — "sex addict."

Our use of the term "sex addict" throughout this material refers to the survival personality of one that is caught in the grip of addiction and is still in denial of the problem, whether through rebellion or ignorance.

The ultimate desire of the Life More Abundant recovery program is to remove the hold of this dominant personality (and the addiction it relies on) and help the individual reclaim their true identity in Christ.

Table of Contents

Acknowledgments

Writing can be a lonely pursuit. This book represents many hours spent alone with my thoughts and my computer. Often when the words didn't come easy, my mind would wander to other things that I could be doing, but two things kept drawing my attention back to this project. One of them was gratitude and the other purpose.

Gratitude

I am exceedingly grateful for a God that so lovingly guided my husband and I through the rugged terrain of sexual addiction recovery. I am so thankful that he gives us hope, a way out of our sin and the promise of a life more abundant. He forgives, he heals, he restores. You can't ask for more than that.

I am also thankful for my husband, Bruce, who has taught me so much about courage, perseverance and love.

His journey out of sexual addiction was long and difficult. There were many times when I know he longed to find an easier path. Times when he wondered if true freedom was even possible. Times when he didn't feel he could go another step, but he forced himself to put one foot in front of the other and, in his exhaustion and pain, kept turning to God for the answers.

Today he is truly free from the insidious addiction that once enslaved him. We rejoice together in his victory and celebrate the awesome marriage and tender affection that we now enjoy.

In spite of all we've been through, I am truly blessed to have him as my partner in life and ministry.

I also want to thank all the wives that have come through our doors over the years. They have displayed such grace and strength in dealing with the intensely personal pain and frustration of their husband's struggle. These women are my heros!

Their insatiable desire to understand their husband's battle and their willingness to look at their own stuff has blown me away. It is out of their mouths and hearts that the majority of the questions in this book have come.

I am grateful, too, for the encouragement they have been to me personally and to the ministry that God has created. I love you all and pray that God will continue to bless each one of you. You're awesome!

Purpose

"Praise be to the God and Father of our Lord Jesus Christ, the Father of compassion and the God of all comfort, who comforts us in all our troubles, so that we can comfort those in any trouble with the comfort we ourselves receive from God."—2 Corinthians 1:3-4

We have received so much. With so much to be grateful for, how can we keep it to ourselves? We want other couples to find the comfort and freedom that we have found. We want *you* to know that there *is* hope.

Forward

Janet Wheeler's *When Sex Causes Heartbreak* addresses many questions that are often asked when sexual sin enters a marriage. My husband, Clarence and I have been doing marriage ministry for nearly 30 years and have seen countless couples struggle with affairs, pornography and the absence of sex in their relationship. Unfortunately, these issues are far too common, leaving couples feeling distressed and hopeless. Our culture would lead us to believe that these behaviors are normal and should either be tolerated or given up on because they are hopeless, not worth saving. As Christians, neither are options. Janet encourages us that *"with God, all things are possible"* and that we serve a powerful Lord.

As a woman faced with my husband's pornography addiction, I have asked many of the questions Janet answers in this book. Now on the other side of his recovery, I wholeheartedly agree with the advice she offers and concur with her encouragement to rely on God. As a result of her first hand experience, Janet knows much of the pain associated with the issue of sexual sin and the efforts involved in moving beyond them. At no point, however, does this author suggest that a woman should "just get over it", but offers Biblical counsel on healing and dealing appropriately with the issues.

While gently handling sensitive matters, Janet calls sin a sin and offers helpful suggestions in dealing with it. She alleviates the misconceptions that these sins of the husband are the fault of the wife. She frequently validates the identity of the offended spouse. Throughout this book, Janet considers the thoughts and feelings that are common to someone betrayed by sexual sins. At the same time, she gives hope that marriages can survive these difficult matters.

When Sex Causes Heartbreak is a valuable resource for women struggling to cope with their husbands' sexual sins. By simply raising the questions, Janet lets women know they are not alone in thinking the way they do. She doesn't stop there though; she offers help and hope with her answers.

My prayer is that every woman struggling with these issues in her marriage will find encouragement in these pages. With the help of Our Lord, I pray that she finds peace, contentment and trust with her husband that may even surpass where it was before the betrayal. As you delve into this book, I encourage you to do so with prayer asking God for an open mind to what He has for your marriage.

Brenda Shuler
BLR: Building Lasting Relationships

Introduction

Few things are as devastating as finding out that your husband struggles with sexual sin. Although my husband was already on the road to recovery by the time I met him, we still encountered many "bumps" in the early days of our marriage.

I know, first hand, the pain of discovering a new stash of pornography; the feeling of distance his acting out put between us; and the excruciating agony of believing that if he was still struggling, I must not be a good enough wife.

Although we're still discovering, every day, what true intimacy is, we now know, from our own experiences that there IS true freedom and hope in Christ Jesus. It is our desire to help other men and women find this truth as well.

It has been interesting to observe that over the years as we've talked with the wives of those struggling with sexual sin, the same questions and frustrations keep popping up. Not surprisingly, many of those questions were exactly the same things I was asking myself a decade or so ago.

When I first began thinking about facilitating a wives' support group many years ago, my attempts to find a good and balanced resource that would help answer those universal questions and provide a basis for traversing this difficult road were extremely disappointing. It was out of that frustration that the idea of developing a resource that would address these challenging issues was born. Written in question and answer format, that little booklet has gone on to help many, many women understand and deal with this unexpected and unwanted intruder in their marriage. The full-length book you are now holding is an expansion of that original 46-page booklet. In addition to the original content, it also provides answers to many more questions that were not considered in the first edition.

I pray that these words will be a light and a comfort to you as you try to comprehend this thing that is wreaking havoc in your most cherished relationship.

It is my desire that you and your family will find the same hope and healing in Jesus Christ that my husband and I have found.

Yes, my soul, find rest in God;
my hope comes from him.
Truly he is my rock and my salvation;
he is my fortress, I will not be shaken.
My salvation and my honor depend on God,
he is my mighty rock, my refuge.
Trust in him at all times, you people;
pour out your hearts to him,
For God is our refuge.

— Psalm 62:5-8

Dealing with the Feelings

There is a time for everything . . .
a time to weep and a time to laugh,
a time to mourn and a time to dance . . .

- Ecclesiastes 3:1,4

Q I only recently found out about my husband's sexual behavior. At first I didn't want to believe it, but it looks like it's true. My emotions are all over the board. How can I begin to come to terms with all these conflicting feelings?

A Whether your spouse has willingly admitted his inappropriate sexual behavior or you have "stumbled" on it through a series of painful discoveries, a disclosure of this nature does bring up a mass of confusing emotions.

Denial, minimization, and blame are normal "first feelings," but other intense emotions quickly follow behind them. Depending on the details of your situation you may feel:

- afraid
- angry
- betrayed
- withdrawn
- rejected
- disgusted
- guilty
- jealous
- depressed
- powerless

or any number of other disturbing feelings. As strange as it may seem, if you have intuitively sensed that something has been wrong in your marriage, you may even have feelings of relief to finally have a "name" for your suspicions.

As Christians we often feel that we have no right to entertain the emotions that well up inside us. Unfortunately, disregarding and denying the things we are experiencing creates a very explosive situation. When we attempt to ignore our feelings, we eventually implode on ourselves through physical sickness or self-hatred, or the repressed emotions turn into deep-rooted anger and bitterness that will find release when and where we least expect it.

It is important to acknowledge what you are feeling to yourself and to God. There is no other way to get past these intense feelings but through them.

God is not afraid of our emotions. Above all he wants us to be real with him and to offer our fears and frustrations to him so he can carry them for us.

Q **I feel so alone and ashamed. Does anybody understand (or even care) how I feel?**

A Spouses whose husbands are involved in some type of sexual misconduct may well be among the loneliest people on the planet. Much of the time these women either know or strongly suspect that their husbands are involved in behavior that they can neither stomach nor comprehend. The nature of the activity often causes their husbands to become secretive and emotionally distant from them. To make matters worse, there is seldom anyone they feel they can talk to about it.

In spite of how you feel, you are not alone. Recent studies indicate that one out of every four Christian couples will experience the pain of an affair and an estimated 30-40% percent of Christian men (and an increasing number of women) struggle with some sort of sexual compulsion or addiction that is negatively affecting their daily life. It is very likely that other women in your immediate circle of friends are struggling with exactly what you are struggling with. But, because of the awkwardness and shame that surrounds the subject, nobody's talking about it . . . especially in the Christian community.

The good news is that there is a growing awareness that sexual immorality is an immense problem, even in our churches. Pioneering work by Dr. Patrick Carnes, Dr. Mark Laaser, Michael Dye and others are helping us gain a new understanding of the motivation behind these sinful sexual expressions.

Out of this understanding new books, teaching and therapy groups are being created to help those that struggle with sexual sin *and* those who love them. Programs like Life More Abundant Network in Washington State, Faithful & True workshops in Michigan,

Heart to Heart Counseling in Colorado and national programs from XXX Church, The Genesis Process and many others are helping strugglers and their spouses find support, healing and marital reconciliation.

It is important for your peace of mind and personal healing that you have with someone you can talk freely with about your own struggle.

This person needs to be someone who:

- will keep your conversations confidential
- loves you as a person and doesn't just see you as a project
- understands addiction and/or persevering through struggles that may not just go away overnight
- is comfortable with the expression of emotions and doesn't require that you conceal yours
- will really listen and encourage you and not just try to "fix" everything with a quick scripture or Christian cliche
- is realistic and won't minimize or awfulize your situation
- has the patience to stand with you as long as it takes

If you are unable to find a friend or pastor that seems to fit the bill, we strongly encourage you to seek out a support group or counselor that specializes in helping those affected by a spouse's sexual addiction.

Q I'm not feeling much of anything. Is that normal? Does it mean I'm doing OK?

A It is common to feel *something* when you experience a personal loss or the betrayal of someone that you trusted. Discovering your husband's struggle embodies *both* of these difficult scenarios. Most people in your situation feel anger, hurt, embarrassment or any number of other emotions. When we aren't experiencing "expected" emotions, it is very often because deep down we're afraid of the sheer magnitude of all there is to feel. Our body and mind are overwhelmed. We are scared of the loss of control, embarrassment, pain, or whatever else we think we may encounter if we let our feelings bubble to the surface.

When we find ourselves in any situation that is particularly painful or threatening to our sense of security, an automatic fight, flight or freeze reaction kicks in. Fight behaviors give us the perception of being in control of the situation and cause other people to back away which helps us feel safe again. But if, for whatever reason, we aren't a fighter, we will naturally gravitate toward finding some way to avoid the issue and its corresponding emotions, altogether.

Those who lean toward flight may run away from the issue by getting overly busy, running to addictive behaviors, exercising or working compulsively, overeating (especially foods with high levels of sugar or fat), excessive drinking or drug use, or escaping into reading, TV or video games.

People who tend to freeze, simply shut down, numb out and pretend that the incident never happened. They may try to avoid expected pain by constantly intellectualizing or analyzing the situation, convincing themselves it is someone else's problem or fault, or hiding their anger (sometimes even from themselves) behind a facade of peace and love. Both flight and freeze are forms of denial. Either one of them will effectively suppress or bury painful or scary emotions.

Since suppressing emotions keeps us from being able to acknowledge and work through the issues that caused them, they don't go away. They stay just below the surface and cause all kinds of other problems which may include illness, lack of energy, over-reactions and low self-esteem.

Stuffing emotions in this way requires much more energy than you might imagine. It is much like trying to hold a beach ball under the water. It gets harder and harder as the minutes tick by until eventually the ball catapults uncontrollably out of the water and out of your hands. Over time our unfelt emotions react similarly. They become increasingly more difficult to keep down and may begin to cause fatigue, lethargy or even depression. Eventually, like the beach ball, those repressed emotions will erupt in a way and time we cannot control.

It is essential for your own well-being that you allow yourself to get in touch with your underlying emotions. Some ways to start include:

- Make a list of what you have lost because of your husband's problem (ie: security, trust, innocence, joy, your ability to hold your head up in public . . .)

- Resist the urge to turn to something else to distract you if thoughts do begin to surface. Sit with them.

- Give yourself permission to feel, to cry, to yell.

Q I feel betrayed and dirty. Will I ever feel good about myself again?

A The truth is, no matter what people say or what you feel, you are not the cause of your husband's sin. You did not "push" him into the arms of another woman or force him to use pornography as a means of sexual release. These are bad choices that he made on his own. Even if you made mistakes as a wife, it did not give him license to sin.

Your husband's actions have shaken the very core of your existence. At the moment you discovered his infidelity you, unavoidably, lost many things that were very precious to you. Your losses may have included:

- trust in him, yourself and the world
- intimacy and integrity in your marriage
- your own dignity, reputation and, perhaps, even friends
- your illusion of how good your marriage was and how special you were to your partner.
- time with your children due to a preoccupation with his issues

In addition, you may also have very real fears about losing:

- your marriage to divorce
- your health to STDs, HIV or other illnesses

You cannot truly forgive your husband until you have counted the costs and allowed yourself to grieve the things that have been taken from you. Once that has happened you can begin to make choices that will release him to God and take away some of the fear and condemnation that you feel. Obviously, there is no guarantee that your husband will be willing to face what he has done, but your earnestness in trying your best and working toward building a healthier relationship is an important part of your own spiritual growth and emotional healing.

Even if it's too late for your marriage and your husband decides he is unwilling to do the work required to understand why he made the choices that he did, you can experience healing, new understanding and a deeper passion for God.

No matter what your husband does or doesn't do, God has a plan for you. . . and it is GOOD! (Jeremiah 29:11)

Q **My husband's actions really hurt me. How do I stop feeling like a victim and make positive steps toward my own healing and growth?**

A

To be honest, you are only a victim if you decide to be. There is no doubt that this is very likely one of the most difficult things you will ever go through. You didn't choose it and you certainly didn't deserve it. But, it is not the end of your story. You will never be the same—but it shouldn't automatically be assumed that it will be a bad thing. Elizabeth Kubler Ross, who in her ground-breaking work with terminally ill patients developed the theory of the five stages of grief, once wrote:

> *The most beautiful people we have known are those who have known defeat, known suffering, known struggle, known loss, and have found their way out of the depths.*
>
> *These persons have an appreciation, a sensitivity and an understanding of life that fills them with compassion, gentleness and a deep loving concern.*

Although it may be of little comfort to you right now, be assured that God will not waste a minute of your pain. If you allow him, he will take this thing that the enemy meant to destroy you and your family and use it to make you even more beautiful.

Letting yourself slip into victim thinking will block that process and cheat you out of the blessings that God wants to provide.

Any time we allow ourselves the "luxury"of wallowing in self-pity, blaming, or fixating on what others have done to us and how everyone else has it so much better than we do, we risk having that victim mentality become a chronic condition that keeps us from seeing or accepting solutions or positive opportunities in our lives.

As difficult as it can be at times, it is important for our own well-being that we take captive our thoughts and put our efforts into the things that we have the power to control. Doing what we *are* able to do and not wasting energy on what we *aren't*, will bring us to a healthier place and keep us from sinking into hopelessness.

THE CHOICES ARE YOURS

I CAN CONTROL . . .

MY feelings, thoughts & behaviors

. . . so . . .
IF I CHOOSE TO ACT ON THEM. . .

I can gain mastery over my life

"Working on our own stuff" enables us to make better choices and feel good about ourselves.

I CAN'T CONTROL . . .

Family dynamics or the thoughts, feelings or behaviors of others

. . . but . . .
IF I CHOOSE TO ACT ON THEM ANYWAY. . .

I become codependent, enabling &/or caretaking which feels hopeless, helpless, angry, frustrated, out of control, crazy, depressed

Trying to do the impossible leads to a ceaseless cycle of striving with no success.

BOUNDARIES

I CHOOSE

I CHOOSE

. . . but . . .
IF I CHOOSE NOT TO ACT. . .

I will feel hopeless, helpless, angry, frustrated, out-of-control, crazy, depressed, confused.

The passive approach leads to a learned helplessness that blinds us to our choices.

. . . so . . .
IF I CHOOSE NOT TO ACT. . .

I can let go & let God take care of it.

"God, grant me the serenity to accept the things I cannot change; the courage to change the things I can, & the wisdom to know the difference."
—*Reinhold Niebuhr*

SELF-PITY

Q **My husband says he still loves me, but how can he love me and still do the things he does?**

A Most sexual activity is not about the actual physical sex act at all. In a healthy relationship it is about vulnerably sharing our innermost selves and feeling oneness with our partner. When used inappropriately, sexual arousal and release are used to fill our needy places and anesthetize the pain in our lives.

Our brain is interesting. It has, built into it, a survival instinct. When something happens to make us feel afraid or uncomfortable it immediately seeks anything that will take those feelings away and make us feel right again. When our brain begins to associate a certain activity with helping us to regain "normalcy", the seeds of an addiction are sown.

Events come through our senses—seeing, hearing, smelling, tasting, touching—to a part of our brain called the limbic system. This is where they are processed and tagged as safe or dangerous.

The limbic system has no sense of time, so if it experiences a familiar feeling that is associated with past trauma—like fear or rejection—this part of the brain recognizes it as a sign of danger and immediately creates a craving for the thing that has helped us survive and feel normal before. For many men pornography, compulsive masturbation, sexual fantasy, or the rush of winning over a new woman becomes this normalizer.

Unfortunately, when we are in this limbic "survival mode" the cognitive thinking/reasoning part of our brain—the part that understands how much our actions will hurt our loved ones; the part that knows right from wrong; the part that is moral and loving—actually shuts down. Our brain only knows is that we are in physical or emotional danger and need to get back to normal . . . now!

Your husband may love you very deeply, but when, because of past trauma, his brain tells him that he is in danger, he ceases to be able to think normally and, instead, can only react to the situation in the way that his brain has been programmed. It is this continual shifting between the cognitive reasoning brain and the reactive limbic brain that produces the Jekyll and Hyde double life indicative of a sex addict.

Q **It's strange. It seems like I've been sick a lot more than usual since finding out about my husband's problem. Do you think there's any connection?**

A We are complex triune beings—body, mind, and spirit. Our physical bodies *are* dramatically affected by our emotions. Unresolved negative emotions can create a kind of perpetual stress that has actually been shown to reduce our immune system. In fact, many experts believe that 75-90% of all visits to primary care physicians are directly related to stress.

A number of common emotions have the potential to create stress and trigger serious disease:

- **Anger, hostility** or **repressed anger** are often linked to hypertension, coronary artery disease, tension and migraine headaches, chronic back pain, TMJ and fibromyalgia.

- **Anxiety** and **fear** often lead to irritable bowel syndrome, panic attacks, mitral valve prolapses and heart palpitations.

- **Resentment, bitterness, unforgiveness** or **self-hatred** can cause autoimmune disorders, rheumatoid arthritis, lupus and multiple sclerosis.

- **Guilt** and **shame** increase incidences of depression (which can ultimately lead to heart disease, osteoporosis and cancer).

Depending on your individual situation you may be feeling intense levels of any one, or even several of these emotions. All of them, even if they are ignored or repressed, create the kind of stress that affects the very cells of your body.

Tension headaches and stomach, intestine, bowel or skin problems are often early signs that stress is affecting our bodies. If we simply medicate these symptoms instead of addressing the source of the stress, they can become chronic and other problems like sleeplessness, weight loss or gain and muscle aches may begin to show. Left unchecked it can ultimately lead to fatigue, depression and accelerated aging, as well as cancer, arthritis and other types of serious chronic illness.

The only way to stop these snowballing affects is to acknowledge your emotions, feel them and release them. These activities may help you begin that process:

- **Check your attitude** - Deadly emotions are created or exacerbated by our attitudes. You *choose* how you think and respond to the situations in your life.

- **Engage with yourself, God and others** - Admit what you're feeling, love yourself, acknowledge God's presence, cast your cares on Him and voice your decision to trust Him. Make the choice to be loving to others and accept their love for you.

- **Replace distorted thinking with truth** - Your thoughts create your emotions. Watch out for automatic negative thinking. Let God and others help you find the truth.

- **Forgive** - Forgiveness releases buried anger, resentment, bitterness, shame, grief, guilt, hate and other toxic emotions.

- **Lighten up** - As hard as it may be right now, cultivate joy and laughter. Extended elevations of stress hormones like Cortisol act like acid in the body, especially affecting the brain and memory. Once these levels rise it's difficult to lower them medically. Laughter is one of the few things that seems to help.

- **Learn to relax** - take a mini-break from daily stresses with activities like deep breathing, meditation and prayer, aerobic exercise, massage and good sleep.

I feel stuck. How can I get over all the hurt, betrayal, and loss I'm still feeling?

A God gave us three tools that will help resolve most of the issues in our lives that can keep us stuck:

1. Forgiveness . . . *to resolve the hurt caused by others*

Derived from two Greek words: Charisma (gift) and Aphesis (letting go), forgiveness is giving someone the gift of letting go of the resentments and anger that were created by their hurtful words or actions. It blesses both of us. If we hang on to the resentments caused by our wounding, it's like drinking poison and expecting the other person to die. *We* receive the greater harm.

When we forgive, we transfer the responsibility of making them "get" what they've done over to God and get out of His way so He can work in both their lives and ours. It's a choice that sets us free to experience relief, release and peace and finally let our hurts heal.

It's not a feeling. It's not forgetting, excusing, condoning or pretending it didn't hurt. It's saying it *did* happen, it hurt me and it *wasn't* OK, but I am deciding to turn it over to God to handle in whatever way HE sees fit. It's a transaction between us and God that requires no participation from the wounder. It's *not* reconciliation. That can only happen when the wounder realizes what they did, apologizes from the heart and takes steps to make sure it never happens again.

2. Repentance . . . *to free us when WE did something wrong*

Just like those that hurt us, we hurt others in many ways. Sometimes we do it intentionally. Selfishly. We say something that cuts to the bone. We gossip. We ignore another person's needs or requests. Other times we do it by accident. We forget to do what we've promised. We're careless. We hide things. We lie to protect ourselves, not thinking of the impact it will have on others.

Even though, *we* were fully responsible for the way things turned out, God still gives us a way to resolve our mistakes. We aren't doomed to live forever with the broken relationships, guilt, and regrets. He provides a way to make it right. First we must humble ourselves and become vulnerable by admitting to the one we harmed (whether it be man or God) that we messed up. Then we need to repent for our hurtful words or actions. We must lay down our own will and self-interest and refocus on God's desires and direction in our life.

Confession and repentance cleanse us deep within and provide a way to put those damaging encounters behind us. We no longer need to be controlled by our shame. We are, once again, free—free to experience God's peace.

3. Grieving . . . *to deal with the loss of anything important to us*

Most people automatically associate "grief" with the death of a special person, pet or relationship but, in truth, grieving is necessary whenever we are deprived by choice or by chance, of *anything* we have cherished deeply. It doesn't matter what or who has been lost, we must go through the grieving process before we can truly accept the loss and find serenity and peace of mind.

Losses come in many forms. They can be tangible things like a cherished keepsake or a valuable possession, or they can be virtually invisible like the loss of a dream, a relationship, a freedom, an identity or a purpose. They may have their source in recent situations or in long ago childhood trauma and deprivations.

The effects of these losses will never go away until they are resolved in our heart and mind. Time alone does not heal. Grieving is the intentional process of giving honor and saying goodbye to something that was important to you. It releases us from the bondage of the past so we can finally begin to enjoy new relationships, traditions, and dreams.

Is It Addiction?

I do not understand what I do.
For what I want to do I do not do,
but what I hate, I do.

- Romans 7:15

Q Is it possible that MY husband is a sex addict?

A Not all inappropriate sexual behaviors are indicative of sexual addiction. Having an affair or occasionally using pornography does not automatically classify someone as a sex addict. While all non-marital sexual activity is outside of God's will, and qualifies as sexual sin, it is not necessarily addictive.

Addiction specialists agree that certain elements must be present for a substance or behavior to be considered addictive. These elements include:

1. Compulsion
Romans 7:21-23 talks about desiring one thing but being compelled to do another. Addiction robs people of their ability to make choices about their behavior and drives them to do the very thing they vowed not to do.

2. Obsession
Addicts eventually become so preoccupied with their addiction that they start to ignore work, family, hobbies, and other areas of their life to focus almost solely on their addictive cycle.

3. Persistence
This is the most undeniable sign that a person is struggling with an addiction. Even when an addict faces extremely dire consequences because of their actions, they are powerless to stop the behavior that led to that negative outcome for any length of time.

4. Tolerance
Addictive behavior is also governed by the rule of diminishing returns. This means that as time goes by it takes more and more of the behavior to get the same "high" or feeling of relief.

If these indicators are present in relation to your husband's sexual behavior, it is highly likely that he is a sex addict. Many wives are shocked to discover that their spouse has been leading a secret life "under their nose" for years. His shame and the belief that his addiction is what helps him survive, has significantly honed his ability to hide his behavior from her.

Q What exactly is sexual addiction?

A Sexual addiction is one of the most misunderstood of all compulsions. Even many professionals do not fully understand its root and treatment. The truth is, sexual addiction is not a thirst for sex at all. It is a thirst for God —for true intimacy with the Creator and his creation. When we are abused or abandoned at a young age, our ability to trust in people, and even God, is diminished. We become too afraid to strive for the true intimacy that our heart yearns for. Instead, we seek to substitute a false intimacy of our own creation—an illusion that we believe will give us what we need without having to risk the pain that we are convinced would come from daring to trust others.

If we discover that something like sexual activity numbs our fears and masks our internal pain, our brain tags it as being something that can make us feel "normal" again. When we experience pain or fear later on, our body remembers and starts to crave the very thing that diminished those feelings before. The more we choose that activity over running to God, the more ingrained it becomes. It becomes our idol—the thing that we rely on to get us through the hard times. As it gains more and more place in our hearts, we increasingly move away from the source of life toward the death that addiction brings.

Addiction is unique in that it destroys the whole person. Every aspect of our being (physical, mental, emotional, spiritual and social) is affected. As our thinking becomes increasingly distorted, sexually compulsive rituals can become synonymous with power (feeling in control), adequacy (feeling good enough) and love. But, no matter how much sex an addict gets, it is never enough to fill the void in their heart. Each encounter leaves them feeling even more empty and alone. Only God can fill our empty places—anything else will eventually let us down.

The chart on the facing page illustrates the normal cycle of addiction. Most strugglers have periods where they are somewhat behavior free, but, without true healing, they are only able to maintain their "sobriety" until some trigger event puts pressure on their internal pain. It surprises most people, even the addicts themselves, to find out that the actual triggers aren't short skirts and cleavage. They are almost always non-sexual events relating to an individual's internal belief system. Common triggers include things like the fear of rejection, injustice, or feeling inadequate or helpless.

The event and the potential pain it brings sends the addict into an emotional tail-spin and awakens the limbic brain—the part of the brain that is in charge of making the addict feel safe again. It creates a craving for the things that have made them feel normal before and temporarily disables the cognitive brain with its morals and rational thinking so it won't get in the way of what it believes needs to be done.

With the help of the limbic brain, the addict then begins to make the choices necessary to override their conscience and move ever closer to acting out. Distorted thinking, rituals and finally the acting out itself, cause calming hormones to be released in the addict's body that begin to make them feel safe and in control once again. Once that safe feeling has been restored, the limbic survival brain relinquishes control and the cognitive brain once again takes over.

It is at this point that the addict realizes what they have just done and begins to feel the full onslaught of remorse, self-disgust and guilt about their moral failure and broken promises. Their despair is real and intense and they face, once again, a set of difficult choices. Without God's help the addict naturally moves toward self-hatred; blame or false hope, and another new cycle. Only surrender—the most difficult choice—will provide a different outcome.

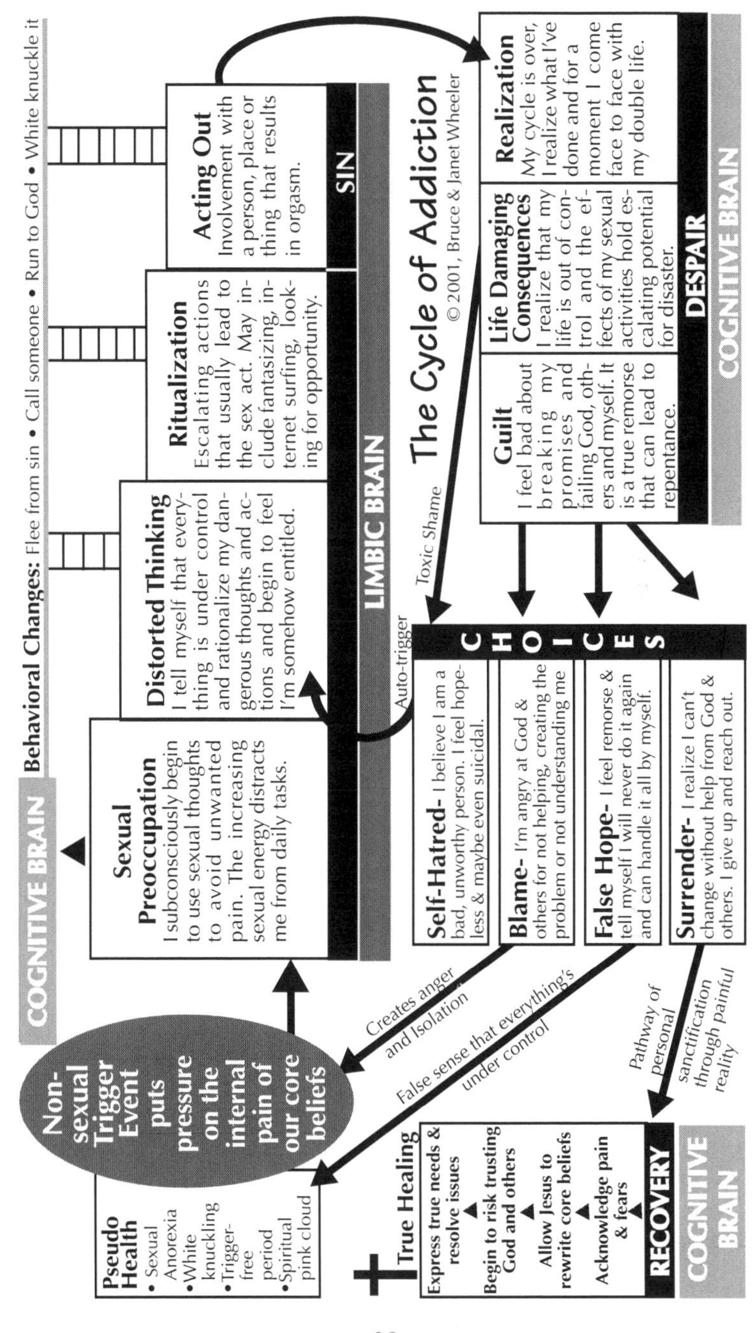
Behavioral Changes: Flee from sin • Call someone • Run to God • White knuckle it
COGNITIVE BRAIN
Sexual Preoccupation
I subconsciously begin to use sexual thoughts to avoid unwanted pain. The increasing sexual energy distracts me from daily tasks.
Distorted Thinking
I tell myself that everything is under control and rationalize my dangerous thoughts and actions and begin to feel I'm somehow entitled.
Ritualization
Escalating actions that usually lead to the sex act. May include fantasizing, internet surfing, looking for opportunity.
Acting Out
Involvement with a person, place or thing that results in orgasm.
SIN
LIMBIC BRAIN
The Cycle of Addiction
© 2001, Bruce & Janet Wheeler
Realization
My cycle is over, I realize what I've done and for a moment I come face to face with my double life.
Life Damaging Consequences
I realize that my life is out of control and the effects of my sexual activities hold escalating potential for disaster.
Guilt
I feel bad about breaking my promises and failing God, others and myself. It is a true remorse that can lead to repentance.
DESPAIR
COGNITIVE BRAIN
Toxic Shame
Auto-trigger
CHOICES
Self-Hatred- I believe I am a bad, unworthy person. I feel hopeless & maybe even suicidal.
Blame- I'm angry at God & others for not helping, creating the problem or not understanding me
False Hope- I feel remorse & tell myself I will never do it again and can handle it all by myself.
Surrender- I realize I can't change without help from God & others. I give up and reach out.
Non-sexual Trigger Event puts pressure on the internal pain of our core beliefs
Creates anger and Isolation
False sense that everything's under control
Pathway of personal sanctification through painful reality
Pseudo Health
• Sexual Anorexia
• White knuckling
• Trigger-free period
• Spiritual pink cloud
True Healing
Express true needs & resolve issues
Begin to risk trusting God and others
Allow Jesus to rewrite core beliefs
Acknowledge pain & fears
RECOVERY
COGNITIVE BRAIN

Once established, addictions do not just go away by themselves. They won't disappear by ignoring them, denying them, or by relying on sheer willpower to stop them. In spite of this, there are many "therapy" methods that promote behavioral change alone.

All too often addicts that have some success at "white knuckling" for a while mistakenly think that they have been healed using the techniques that have been offered, but changing behavior is not the same as true healing. In reality they have only become either walking time bombs, ready to explode back into their addiction whenever the pressures of life break down their stubborn resolve not to act out, or an asexual being that finds a new compulsion like alcohol or drugs, gambling or work to numb them out and reduce their internal aching. Without dealing with the core issues that caused the sexual addiction in the first place the addict will always need something to keep them from feeling their wounds.

Two Roads of Pain

An addict has only two choices and both involve pain. They can:

1. continue acting out knowing that using sex to meet their deep internal needs leads to increasingly destructive behavior and progressively damages their ability to function in personal relationships and grow spiritually in their relationship with God.
2. allow Jesus to help them face the painful memories, fears of rejection and core sinful beliefs and free them from their grip.

True change can only happen when the pain of the addiction becomes greater than the pain of changing.

In Romans 6:14, Paul assures us *"For sin shall not be your master. because you are not under law, but under grace."* God *wants* to deliver us from addiction's grip, but he will not force us to accept his gift of "life more abundant." It's ours to choose or reject.

Q What causes addiction?

A As mentioned earlier in the book, the Limbic System controls both the emotions and the body's automatic survival responses. When we are in a state of fear, the limbic system acts independently from our conscious minds to tell us whether to fight, run, or freeze.

Drugs, alcohol, and even sexual behaviors can be programmed into the limbic system as a way of "numbing out" and escaping uncomfortable thoughts and feelings. When faced with a situation or fear that feels familiar, this part of our brain creates cravings for any activity or substance that has helped us survive it in the past. Thus an addiction is created. It is important to remember that addiction is not about getting high, but about getting back to feeling normal (free of stress).

All compulsions are simply ways our body has discovered to dull pain and anesthetize the loneliness created by our false beliefs. Compulsive sexual behavior, for instance, is a by-product of intense unmet needs that have evolved into a serious mistrust of both God and others. It is the addict's best solution for the constant battle between the deep longing for love and the desperate fear that they will be hurt if they get too close to anyone. Having decided that it is not safe to trust others (or even God) the addict unknowingly creates a self-sufficient personality to help him survive. This survival personality's job is to develop and protect coping skills that will help the addict survive in a world they perceive is unsafe.

The personality strives to fortify the walls that keep people from getting too close. It is convinced that it must avoid pain at all cost. This is the part of the addict that learns how to lie to avoid the pain (and shame) of being found out. It minimizes and denies the severity of its actions. It learns how to rationalize and blame others to get the attention off itself.

The addiction, for all practical purposes, becomes the addict's highly protected idol—the thing they rely on instead of God to get them through hard times and difficult situations.

Q Isn't sexual addiction just a lust problem?

A Humans seem to love to label things. We somehow feel more comfortable if everything is safely tucked in an appropriate category. Unfortunately, many things in our lives, including sexual addiction, are much more complicated than that.

Some people categorize sexual addiction as a sin issue, others chalk it up to bad behavior, or inappropriate choices, and still others have it pegged as a "lust" problem. In actuality it is all of those and more. It is somewhat like the old story of the six blind men and the elephant. Each man was introduced to a different part of the elephant and drew their own conclusions of what the beast was like based on their extremely limited experience. The one who felt only its trunk, described the elephant as similar to a snake; another one that touched the pachyderm's leg thought that the animal was more like a tree, and so on. Although each had something to say, none of the six could accurately describe the animal in total by exploring just one small part of the whole.

So it is with sexual addiction. There are many books and programs that look strictly at one facet or another and offer suggestions for conquering the whole by looking at a very finite part of it. Lust is one area that has garnered a vast amount of attention. There is much material available about conquering lust. One very respected Christian organization even talks about love and lust as being the two different "appetites" of sex addicts and other wayward men. They go on to say that, because of these two conflicting desires, these men can have a wonderfully tender sexual experience with their wife one minute and then go out and seek lustful encounters outside the marriage just hours later.

This is a very inaccurate picture of what is actually going on in the hearts and minds of most men—especially sexual addicts. In fact, it is this type of teaching that helps keep many men trapped. After all, if lust is sin and lust is an innate part of the male species, there is very little hope.

In actuality, lust is nothing more than strong desire. We can lust after money, or knowledge, or sex, or a variety of other things. In terms of sex, lust is usually a somewhat self-serving form of sexual desire that falls short of God's *very* best for our relationship, but in itself is not particularly right or wrong. It's how we use it and who we allow to be the object of that lust that determines its sinfulness.

Contrary to much popular teaching, sexual addiction is not an issue of sex or lust or bad choices, or even external behavior. It is about pain and loneliness and fear. It is only as your husband begins to receive healing for the root causes of his addiction, that he will be free to see and understand the healthy ways that God intended sexual desire to be used.

Q **What did I do to get caught in this situation? How did I ever end up in a relationship with an addict?**

A When you realize that you are a partner of a sex addict, it is not unusual to feel that you have somehow been singled out for pain and disappointment. You may feel that you have been dealt a bad hand; become the butt of some cruel joke; or are being justifiably punished for your past sexual indiscretions.

The truth is, however, that it is most often our own brokenness that causes us to attract a man that is broken in this way. This is not to say that we have done anything wrong, or that any part of our husband's problem is our fault. It's just that subconsciously, because of the addict's fear of being hurt, they tend to gravitate toward potential partners that they believe will not reject them.

The most vulnerable women range from naive virgins and strong Christian women that loudly proclaim that they will *never* get divorced, to women who exhibit severe codependent behaviors or a sexual addiction of their own.

Professionals have discovered that the vast majority of the wives of sexual addicts have experienced physical, sexual or emotional abuse in their own childhood and as many as 20% of them are sex addicts themselves. In most cases, wives find that some counseling for their own past issues and present hurt becomes a necessary part of the restoration process.

Like many people in your situation, you may fear that if you "rock the boat" by working on your "own stuff" or start making demands on your husband, your marriage will fall apart and you'll be abandoned and rejected by not only your spouse, but other significant people in your life, as well.

You must remember that it is just as likely that you will become one of the instruments by which God brings healing and hope to your husband and your marriage. In addition, you will inevitably gain insights about yourself and grow closer to the Lord as you reach out for help and rely on Him for the strength to get you through this period of your life.

There are no guarantees that your husband will ultimately decide that he wants freedom from the grip of addiction, but the only one you can really do anything about is yourself. No matter what happens, you can still live a victorious life with God's help.

Q My brother-in-law says he struggled with pornography in college, but was able to stop without too much effort when he married my sister. How come my husband can't just quit too?

A There could be any number of reasons your husband is having trouble stopping his unwanted behaviors, but there are two key factors that significantly impact a person's ability to "just stop:"

1. **the brain part that generates the craving for sexual activity**

   It is important to differentiate between a habit and an addiction. Many men use pornography and masturbation to relieve boredom, elevate their mood, or because they believe that they *must* have, or are entitled to, regular sexual release. Not all of these users are addicts. Most of this group are making a cognitive choice to pursue their behaviors. They are more likely to struggle with a habit and not an addiction, since the pre-frontal cortex—the thinking/reasoning part of their brain—is responsible for these types of choices.

   Habits—especially long term ones—can be difficult to change, but with diligence and determination, it is generally quite possible even without outside intervention.

   If, however, sexual activity has been recruited by their *limbic* survival brain as a means of dealing with the difficulties of life and avoiding the discomfort of past wounds, behavioral change and willpower will rarely be enough to curb their behavior. Automatic cravings for sexual diversions will continue to be generated every time the limbic brain senses that it is in any type of emotional or physical danger.

2. **the age an individual becomes involved with pornography**

The second factor that seems to have significant impact on someone's ability to "just stop" is the age they start using pornography or other sexually charged pursuits.

It is similar to boiling an egg, If the egg cracks very early in the cooking process, much of the egg white will ooze out of the crack in the shell and create a very deformed looking egg.

If, however, the egg cracks right before it is done cooking there will be little or no distortion because the egg is already nearly solid—full formed—at the time the break happens.

In the same way, when a child starts looking at porn at a very young age—say 8 or 9 or even earlier—their emotional structure is not very well established. They are still figuring out who they are and where they fit in this world, so as they grow up with porn as an integral component in their life, it becomes woven into the very fabric of their being. Without a solid foundation and sufficient life experiences to have provided them with other more helpful coping skills, porn is highly likely to become part of that child's emotional survival arsenal.

On the other hand, if they get involved with porn later in life, because of the pressure to be like their peers or as a way to de-stress during college, they are already much more formed as human beings. Their morals and values are more established. They have more experiences in problem solving and general life skills. Porn or strip clubs or phone sex may be exciting, pleasurable or mood altering, but their more matured inner being is much less likely to become hopelessly entangled in them. It is more of an add-on to life instead of a part of their core being. It can still be very destructive to their life and relationships, and they may begin to see some of the indicators of addiction, but they are likely to find the recovery process to be shorter than those who started at a young age.

Help Me Understand

For wisdom will enter your heart,
and knowledge will be pleasant to your soul.
Discretion will protect you,
and understanding will guard you.

- Proverbs 2:10-11

Q **Why isn't he attracted to me? What's the matter with me?**

A This is not a problem with you. Sexual addiction is an intimacy disorder. Whether he understands it or not, your husband desperately wants to be known and loved. His past experiences, however, have made him extremely afraid of being transparent with people. In his mind, trust and vulnerability *always* lead to pain and rejection.

As his wife, you simultaneously represent his largest want *and* his largest fear. In loving you, he has trusted you more than he has trusted most people. But, still, there is a part of him that is convinced that, if he lets you get too close and see who he really is, you will reject him. True intimacy is too dangerous to risk because his potential loss is too great.

To ensure his "safety," the sex addict substitutes sexual activity for the real love that he yearns for. To make that substitution he must "cleanse" sex of all risk by removing the emotional component.

Pornography is safe. He can turn it on, turn it off or flip the page. He has total control over it. It cannot reject him. Prostitutes are safe. The risk of rejection is minimized by the fact that she is being paid for her services. Even anonymous sex is safe, if it is solely a physical act, devoid of "emotional attachment."

When sex is with a person they care about, however, emotions ARE involved. Many addicts fear that if they don't "perform" they will also be rejected, so they develop a "robot" that methodically carries out their husbandly duty as an almost "out of mind" experience. In these situations their thoughts are lost safely in fantasy or numbness—only the physical shell is actually going through the motions. Other addicts find even this tactic to be too scary and shut down their sexuality altogether.

Either way, there is a lot of pain and emptiness in not being loved in the way that God intended you to be. It is difficult to remember that this is not about you personally. It is about *his* inability to trust and risk.

Q **Am I making too big of a deal about this? Wouldn't the problem just go away if I was thinner, sexier or had a stronger sex drive?**

A This IS a big deal. Although it may sound somewhat melodramatic, your husband's intimacy disorder is no less damaging to him than a cancerous tumor or a bad heart. The disease of addiction will ultimately cost him his life, whether literally or by simply commandeering his every waking moment. Experts tell us that 71% of addicts have contemplated suicide as their only hope of finally ending their addictive cycle. Many more addicts risk life-threatening disease through affairs and prostitutes.

No matter how much you want it to, your husband's problem will never go away on its own or because you try to be something you are not. Nothing goes away until it is resolved and addiction can not be resolved by external changes like weight loss or suggestive clothing.

Because of our God-given desire to be seen as lovely, it is easy for us to jump to the conclusion that we have somehow missed the mark and brought this situation on ourselves, especially if we are feeling unattractive, or ashamed because we have gained a little (or a lot of) weight. It certainly doesn't help that other people (even the "professionals" and our own husbands) point the finger at us as "the reason." If we are already beating ourselves up about our inadequacies it is easy to gravitate toward, and even embrace, comments that confirm our negative feelings about ourselves.

Addicts continually search for anything that will take the focus off of themselves. Few things work better than telling a wife that is doubtful about her attractiveness that he wouldn't have to go elsewhere if she hadn't "packed on the pounds" or was a little more sexually exciting. Ironically, even stick thin models, gorgeous Hollywood stars and other beautiful women struggle with "not measuring up" in their addicted spouse's eyes.

The addict usually doesn't intend to be mean or hurtful, they are just subconsciously doing and saying anything that will direct the attention away from them and keep them from having to accept the responsibility for their actions.

Just remember that, no matter what anyone says, you are not the cause of the addiction—your husband's heart was wounded and the stage set for addiction long before you came into the picture.

Q **Wouldn't it be better to just ignore my husband's problem? I really don't think I want to know what he's doing.**

A Some women intentionally choose to put their head in the sand. They purposefully don't look at their husband's computer history or ask any questions. A few even tell their husband that they can do whatever they want, as long as *she* never finds out. Somehow they hope that, if they don't look at it, it will just go away on its own or, at the very least, that denying the problem will help keep them from getting hurt.

They believe they're protecting themselves and their marriage. If they don't rock the boat, they won't have to deal with any anger, defensiveness or verbal retaliation. They can just go on about their life oblivious to what their husband is doing. What they're not considering is the potential cost *they* will pay for their decision.

We have talked to many wives over the years. Virtually all of those that have chosen to deal with their husband's issue in any other way but head-on, end up feeling one or more of the following:

1. Ashamed
Maybe you've been able to convince yourself that you can accept the internet pornography, fantasy, or incessant looking at every woman that passes by. It's quite possible that your husband's current level or frequency of questionable activity, although somewhat irritating, is not intolerable. But, the truth is it's not always going to be like it is today. It *will* get worse. Maybe not this month, or even this year, but if he continues to pursue a sexual "solution" to the problems in his life, his behaviors will escalate. Will you still be able to "look the other way" if he, like so many, gets caught looking at pornography

at work; "hooking up" with women he meets in online sex chat rooms; frequenting prostitutes, or participating in some other sort of criminal sexual behavior? The more enmeshed he becomes in this addiction, the greater the likelihood that his behaviors will be observed by someone outside the family.

2. Lonely

As the grip of addiction tightens, the addict becomes increasingly distracted and has less time for family and friends. My husband said that just before he gave up and went for help, he estimates that 98% of his waking hours (and a good share of those he should have been sleeping) were actively spent on his addiction. He had no time left to think about or experience other things in life. He was no longer there for his wife or his children. Even when he was in the same room, his mind was somewhere else, thinking about what he had seen or done or figuring out when and where his next opportunity would be.

Even if it never gets *that* bad, every secret your husband keeps, whether by his own choice or your request, is a portion of his soul that becomes walled off from you and others. Even an accumulation of the smallest secrets, will begin to erode any unity you have had in your marriage.

3. Angry

Women who end up spending 20 or 30 years hoping that their husband's problem has run its course, or fluctuating between confronting them and blindly trusting that things have gotten better, usually end up so emotionally worn down that they just can't face the issue any longer. They have nothing left to give. Most regret that they have wasted their best years and settled for a life of disappointment. They feel cheated and resentful, even though their choices helped create the situation they're in.

Very few men are able to reach out for help without an external catalyst. Choosing to confront his issue directly, from the start, provides the best chance for a positive outcome for both of you.

Q If he told me it only happened once or that he used to have a problem but it's over, shouldn't I believe him?

A It is, of course, possible that your husband was "innocently" experimenting with an activity that he had been curious about and had the "bad fortune" of getting caught. It may have been more a case of bad judgement than compulsive behavior (especially if he is younger and still forming his lifelong patterns). Jumping to conclusions will not be helpful to your relationship. On the other hand, none of us are required to blindly believe everything our husband tells us to qualify as a loving, Christian wife. Trust must be earned.

When someone is "caught" and the proof of their sinful behavior is undeniable, they know they have to "fess up" to something. It is easier to "report" than it is to confess. Talking about past struggles distances us from current behavior and soothes our guilt about not telling (or our need to tell). Reporting is also used to "test" reactions. The addict may throw out a bit of information to see how their spouse reacts before they risk disclosing more. If she responds by calling him a pervert or turning away in disgust he knows it's not safe to share any more of his secret world.

One way to address the "should I believe him or not" dilemma is to request that he be totally accountable (ie: finances, phone bill, checkbook, credit card, Internet usage, etc.) for a period of time to prove that it was an isolated incident. The conversation might go something like this: "I love you . . . I want to believe you, but statistics show at least 25% of men have problems with this sort of activity. I need assurances that this was a one time thing. If you are willing to give full disclosure of your finances, etc. to me or someone we both trust, we can, hopefully, put this issue to rest. If, however, we find that you are struggling with a bigger problem, I want you to know that I will still love you, but we will need to find some outside help so it doesn't end up destroying you or our relationship."

It is important to remember that, if they do have a deeper problem, the addict will try desperately to protect what they believe is the thing that helps them survive in this world. Lying and redirecting the conversation often become an important part of that protection mechanism.

Q **He says he loves the Lord. If that's so, shouldn't he be free from struggling?**

A As much as we might like it to be so, it is rare that all of our struggles go away the minute we acknowledge Jesus Christ as our Savior. Sometimes we forget (or are never taught) that there is a difference between salvation and sanctification. Salvation is a free gift that is guaranteed to all who turn their lives over to God. Sanctification, however, is a lifelong process of changing to become more like Christ.

It is similar to going to a new doctor that you've been told is an expert in treating physical problems like the one you have been experiencing. It is not merely meeting the doctor that heals you, it is the process he takes you through that brings you back to health. Much of that process involves his capable diagnosis and knowledge of appropriate treatment, but sometimes there are things that we must do, under his guidance, to aid in the recovery.

The Great Physician also knows what is required for our complete healing and freedom from those things that torment us. Although He has every ability to heal us instantly, he often asks us to go through a process to get to that place of healing.

More than anything, God wants a relationship with us. He knows that it is our weaknesses that force us to turn to him and it is in that turning that we learn to trust him and let his divine strength replace our human frailties. He allows some of our struggles to remain for a season to help direct us to him and his sovereign power. It is through the recovery *process* that we really begin to know our Creator and our God in an intimate way and allow his abundant grace to be sufficient to meet our needs and fill our empty spots.

The fact that your husband is still struggling has nothing to do with whether he loves the Lord or not. It has everything to do with his ability and willingness to risk trusting God with his fears—fears that are often so deeply imbedded and so long denied that he may not even be aware of them himself until he begins to allow God to bring them to the surface.

Q **Why do some men have affairs and others use pornography?**

A

The answer to this question is as varied as the men that participate in these activities. There does seem to be some correlation, however, with the type of wounding they received earlier in their lives. Simply put . . .

Mother Wound

If a mother is an abusive, rage-aholic, a small boy might make the internal decision that women aren't safe and can't be trusted.

Later when hormonal changes and natural curiosity kick in, this belief may make this young man look for "safe ways" to experiment with sexuality. These might include masturbation and pornography, as well as phone sex and internet chat rooms that guarantee a safe distance between themselves and women that they decided long ago are unpredictable and dangerous.

Father Wound

If the father is abusive or absent, the mother may become "everything" to the young boy—his protector, his friend, "a virtual saint." In these cases pleasing mom—the only parent he feels he has left—becomes of paramount importance.

Later in life this man may only feel "normal" and safe when women are pleased with him. Unfortunately, once his limbic system equates the adoration of women with security and survival, his insatiable need for approval and attention may make it difficult to commit to just one woman. Continually craving the approval of women could make him highly susceptible to affairs.

Men with father wounds often take on the role of "God's gift to women" and hone their skills at being suave and debonair to capture the attention of the women they need to affirm them.

Q Why does my husband have such childish attitudes about sex? He frequently makes inappropriate statements and jokes in front of friends and family. He often acts like he's still 14 years old.

A He may actually be stuck at 14 in sexual maturity . . .or even younger. Although addicts appear to be mature adults seeking the ultimate adult pleasures, they are, in actuality, responding as scared children who were never able to develop a strong enough sense of security to be able to risk experiencing real love and intimacy.

At whatever point he began using sexual activity for survival and protection instead of an expression of love, he stopped growing sexually. At that point sex became self-centered. Further exploration as to how to share the experience with someone else became non-important.

Making love was meant to be a "full body" experience. It was created as a total sharing of one another by a committed couple. To that end, it is intended to utilize our entire being—the mind, body and emotions.

In essence by using sex to fill a role other than that of expressing love, the addict reduces it to little more than a physical experience. All focus is diverted to doing what it takes to get to the orgasm. Although they know how to "perform" physically, these men generally have limited understanding of the mental and emotional facets of a sexual relationship. Even their attempts at "making it good for their partner" are most often centered on making themselves feel adequate and safe and not on giving their spouse pleasure.

Addicts do not understand the pleasure and contentment that can come from sharing intimately with another person. The mental and emotional aspects of sex are the parts that make it loving and special and more than "animal attraction." Without them we are left with only a physical manifestation devoid of tenderness, respect, and reciprocation.

One of the most difficult things for the recovering addict is to let go of their "sexual formula" and experience the awkwardness and clumsiness of that 14 year old as they learn how to develop real physical intimacy.

Q **I don't feel like he's really with me when we have sex. It seems automatic and cold. I can't explain it, but it feels icky.**

A It is important to remember that most addicts become addicts because of the conflict between their desperate need to be loved and their terrible fear of being hurt. In order to avoid the pain that they are convinced intimate relationships hold, the sex addict adopts one of two basic strategies:

1. Sexual and emotional avoidance
The addict tries to keep himself safe by sealing off his heart and distancing himself from any physical connection by basically becoming asexual. Not only does this keep him from having to risk being vulnerable and getting hurt, but he may also be able to convince himself that he no longer has a problem since he's not acting out. This tactic can, indeed, be very effective in keeping the addict from acting out, but unfortunately, it also keeps him from having sex with his wife as well.

2. Sexual obsession
Sexual arousal combined with physical closeness (imaginary or real) becomes a substitute for real intimacy. Substituting the sex act for love is a way of connecting while staying protected from the possibility of real relational pain. Fantasizing or using pornography is, understandably, safe since relationship is not required . . . but real people can be unpredictable and, therefore, scary for the addict.

In order to create a sense of security, he may develop an elaborate system (or "formula") for gaining control over himself and any situation that feels "dangerous." Departure from this prescribed pattern can cause him to panic. The addict may rely heavily on his fantasies to help him "perform" and may seldom connect verbally or visually with his "real" partner. As empty and painful as this can be for the wife, it is interesting to note that this robot-like state actually diminishes his sexual pleasure as well. Men report increased sensation and stronger orgasms once they are able to stay present and connect with their wives instead of the fantasies during sex.

Q I tell him I want a romantic evening and he buys some sleazy nightgown or rents some disgusting video. It's so devastating. Why doesn't he "get it"?

A Most addicts have a hard time with the concept of "romantic." Romance involves relationship and, because of their fears, few addicts have a clue about how to have a deep and intimate relationship.

Since many addicts substitute sexual behavior for intimacy, it is only natural for them to substitute images and objects that have been programmed into their minds as "sexy" for the totally alien concept of romance.

He is not trying to disappoint you or degrade you by his actions. He truly doesn't understand what you want, because he has never experienced it. It's as if you're talking in a foreign language, because that is exactly what these concepts are for him. He has no point of reference. He cannot do what he does not know.

He may act totally clueless when you are critical of his attempts. It is not an act. He IS clueless.

If you were suddenly thrust into an operating room and expected to intuitively know what help and tools the doctor needed to complete a complicated surgery, you would, most likely, be at a total loss. Even if the physician asked for a specific tool by name you might not know what he was talking about. If he asked you to go ahead and close up for him, you would probably freeze. So it is for your husband when he is faced with choosing and using the instruments, techniques and knowledge required to show romantic love to his wife.

As disheartening as it is, it will most likely be well into your husband's recovery before he can begin to see and understand what you need.

Patience around this issue is admittedly difficult because it touches your core issues, longings and feelings of self worth. It is important to admit to God and yourself that this is a very painful situation and actually grieve the fact that your desires can not be met as you would like them to be at this time.

Q **Would it be helpful if I joined him in his activities or fantasies?**

Participating in your husband's activities will be detrimental for both of you:

For Your Husband:

His made-up world of sexual images and fantasy help him to stay stuck and hide from the risk of true intimacy. As long as he is encouraged to settle for the counterfeit, he will never have reason to explore the healing process and the possibility of a healthy sexual relationship.

If you are playing out his fantasies, neither one of you are being your true selves. The definition of intimacy is to know and be known. If you are recreating the images in your husband's mind, how will he ever get to know the true you or you him? To find healing, the addict needs to learn who he is sexually. Addictive fantasy will deter this.

For You :

Many women participate in their husband's activities because they feel they have no choice if they want to hold their relationship together. They think that cooperating with their husband's requests will, somehow, help their husbands and enhance their sex life.

At his request, a wife may go with him to a topless or striptease bar, have sex with multiple partners or join him in watching raunchy pornographic videos in the hope that it will improve their relationship. Compromising your moral standards and your own best judgement will, over time, leave you feeling little more than a sex object. Even though some of these activities could be a temporary turn-on on some level, addictive, unloving sex ALWAYS leaves you feeling empty. These activities can never fill your need to be seen and cherished and will, instead, start to kill a part of your authentic self.

Taking on the shame of not only his, but your own actions can lead to a life of fear and self-hatred. This is far from the plan God has for your life.

Is there any hope of ever having the intimate relationship I've longed for?

A God intended for us to be relational beings. Matthew 22:37-39 shows how important God views our relationship with him and with others:

Jesus replied: "'Love the Lord your God with all your heart and with all your soul and with all your mind.' This is the first and greatest commandment. And the second is like it: 'Love your neighbor as yourself.'"

If, however, our early relationships were abusive, neglectful, or otherwise unsafe, we may have decided that people (and maybe even God) could not be trusted. Compulsive sexual behavior is just one of our humanistic solutions for the constant battle between longing to be loved and desperately fearing that we will get hurt if we allow anyone to get too close. Superficial relationships; an over-reliance on online "friendships;" convincing ourselves we don't need anyone; or investing the majority of our time and energy into things or pets instead of people are other ways we may attempt to find connection without risk.

The ability to give and accept love is only possible to the degree a person is able to trust God and others. When we are unable to trust, an intense despair, loneliness and fear of relationship imbeds itself deep into our soul.

Sexual addiction is actually an intimacy disorder. People struggling with it have never learned how, or dared to be, truly intimate with others. But, as they pursue recovery, and their addiction begins to lose its control they will finally be free to address the underlying issues that caused them to close part of themselves off from others.

Although secular therapy has traditionally had only a 3-5% success rate in treating sexual addiction and even the Christian programs that focus solely on behavioral changes have limited permanent results, total healing is *absolutely* available to your husband through Jesus Christ.

The healing of what has fueled the addiction does not instantly solve all of his intimacy issues, however. Eliminating the unwanted behaviors is an essential first step, but it will not automatically create the intimacy you desire. That will grow over time.

God wants us all to experience true intimacy. He wants us to feel genuinely loved and satisfied, but the old feelings and fears that stand in the way will not just fade away on their own. These old issues need to be systematically resolved before we can finally be free of them. Your husband, and perhaps yourself, as well, must be willing to face head-on a lifetime of hurts and fears. Only Jesus can give us the strength, and courage we need to take that risk.

The only way for *any* of us to realize total healing of our broken trust is through the difficult process of allowing Jesus to replace the fears and lies that have ruled our lives with his truth. As this truth permeates our hearts and minds we become increasingly able to trust both God and people and allow them into the innermost places of our lives. The joyous side-effect is that we become free to experience a deep and fulfilling relationship with our spouse.

The challenge for you, as a couple, will not be to *rebuild* the intimacy in your marriage, since one or both of you were actually unable to be truly intimate in the past. Your relationship will require God's *retrofitting.*

In the construction industry, retrofitting is defined as *to furnish with new or modified parts or equipment not available or considered necessary at the time of manufacture.*

Together, with God's help, you will finally be able to learn how to communicate better, share more deeply, and build trust between you. The more you become vulnerable with each other, the closer you will become in body, mind *and* spirit.

Q Why does my husband always seem so angry?

A It is very common for an active addict to display an unusual amount of anger. There is so much for him to be furious about—he may be mad at himself for not being able to beat this thing, mad at God for not saving him from its destruction, mad at society for becoming ever more blatantly sexual, and even mad at the sex trade for continually tempting him. It is normal for his anger to escalate even more in early recovery as he begins to understand that his coping mechanism—the thing that has helped him feel "safe"—is being challenged. Even though it is destroying his life, the thought of living without can seem overwhelmingly dangerous and scary.

When *any* of us—addict or not—feel threatened, unsafe, or scared it is natural to respond with an automatic fight, flight or freeze reaction. If your husband is normally a fighter, his anger may be stronger or more evident than it would be for those who historically run away from their problems, or hunker down, numb out, or veg out to avoid feeling the full onslaught of their internal fear or pain.

Men, for the most part, are much more likely to demonstrate visible anger than women. This is due in part to societal conditioning. Many of these guys grew up in a world that insisted that real men are *always* tough. They may have been raised with a steady stream of messages like "boys don't cry," "there's something wrong with a man that is too emotional" or "don't be a wuss." Anger has, somehow, risen up to be the one "acceptable" emotion for men. It makes them look and feel strong and in control, even when they are feeling anything but that, deep inside.

Because of its uncanny ability to hide our true feelings from those around us, anger is often called a secondary emotion. It effectively keeps people from being aware of the anxiety, shame, sadness, fear, frustration, guilt, disappointment, worry, embarrassment, jealousy or hurt that is really in their hearts.

These underlying primary emotions feel very vulnerable, *especially* for a man. Covering them with a curtain of anger feels much safer and by our society's standards, more "manly." Some forms of anger actually encourage people to back away from us, further insuring that no one will get close enough to discover our real emotions.

It is important to realize, however that not all anger is obvious and explosive. Perfectionism, workaholism and people-pleasing all have their roots in a "yeah, I'll show you" fighting mentality. Sarcasm, back-biting and blaming are also expressions of anger.

Even guilt is nothing more than anger at ourselves for what we did or didn't do. Depression, too, can often find its source in anger that has been turned inward. Resentment, on the other hand, is a thinly veiled anger about what *others* did or didn't do.

Take heart that, no matter what form your husband's anger takes, it will slowly dissipate through the recovery process as he begins to acknowledge and resolve the old issues that created the anger in the first place.

Q **My husband has mentioned having a lot of sexual dreams lately. Should I be worried?**

A Although they can certainly be unsettling, sexual dreams are not unusual for those attempting to move toward freedom. By accessing our subconscious, dreams assist us in examining many of the feelings and experiences that we may find difficult to think or talk about when we're awake. Dreams can help us put words to feelings we have previously been unable to fully acknowledge or explain.

Even without the benefit of formal dream therapy, our dreams can help us define and solve current problems, revisit unresolved issues from the past and explore future possibilities.

There are many theories circulating about the meaning behind various elements in a person's dreams, however we have found that it is much more helpful to focus on the *emotions* in the dream rather than the content. The feelings someone experiences in the dream often hold the key to understanding what their subconscious brain is trying to figure out.

When someone is contemplating or working toward making a change in their life, their subconscious brain starts trying to sort out and understand what's going on. At first it can't figure out why they're not doing the behavior anymore. In the case of addiction, it can't reconcile the fact that they're having triggers and not acting on them. It is not the normal pattern.

Because of this, their dreams may, initially, focus on "completing" the acting out that is no longer being done in real life. The dreams will morph as the individual continues in recovery, but there may be a long period where a significant percentage of his dreams set up some sort of unexpected temptation followed by his failure to resist it. Eventually, though, as his recovery efforts are internalized, there will come a time when he will begin to make wiser choices and even be able to walk away from the temptations in the dreams.

Other dream themes may also be significant. Some may actually provide clues to the non-sexual triggers that fuel your husband's addiction. These might include feeling like a victim, being rejected or overlooked, feeling particularly stressed and overwhelmed, or experiencing out-of-control chaos.

It as very likely that the frequency and vividness of his dreams will decrease as he becomes more and more comfortable in his recovery efforts.

The Shame of it All

Guard my life and rescue me;
do not let me be put to shame, for I take refuge in you.

- Psalm 25:20

Q I talked to my pastor about this once and he basically said "if he's getting it at home, he won't wander." It made me feel awful . . . is it really true?

A These kind of thoughts are based on the erroneous assumption that sexual addiction is about sex. In reality, at the point when your husband realized that sexual activity could make his internal pain go away, it ceased being about sex and became a tool of survival.

Sadly, the church has been slow to grasp the difference between sex as an act of intimate love and sexual activity that serves only as a means for "zoning out", feeling adequate, or decreasing internal agitation and fear. It is unfortunate that both activities have been labeled "sex" because they are very different pursuits stemming from very different motivations.

The prevalent thinking in most churches is still that a good wife who "gives her husband enough" doesn't have to worry about her spouse having affairs or using pornography. It is commonly believed that, if he is fully satisfied at home, he will not venture out to get his "needs" met elsewhere. It is not at all unusual for the wife of a straying husband to be given a lecture on "her duty" or advice on how to be more "exciting."

These accusations, whether spoken or not, have devastating effects on a woman's self-esteem. The wives of sex addicts often feel even greater shame than the addicts themselves. The very nature of the problem seems to implicate them as a contributing factor. The reality is that even in a situation where the wife's brokenness keeps her from "being there" for her husband in a sexual way, her healing (although desirable) would not change the circumstances or her husband's behaviors.

Insinuating that his problems are because she is lacking in the bedroom is a cruel lie that places countless women under a tremendous burden of guilt and prevents them from seeking the counsel and support they need. In fact, the shame and general misunderstanding of sexual addiction, even by professionals, makes it difficult for women to find a safe place to share their overwhelming grief and fear. It is only by surrounding herself with people who understand addiction that a woman can receive the freedom from condemnation that God desires for her.

Q **My husband says its all my fault.**

A As we mentioned on the page that addresses "What Causes Addiction," past experiences have lead most addicts to believe that it is not safe to trust God or the people around them. Because they are convinced that they can't count on anyone else, they develop a self-sufficient personality that will help them survive in a world that feels rejecting and unsafe.

When the survival personality finds something that seems to alleviate the pain of the addict's unmet needs, its role changes to protector of this activity. Unfortunately, this protection often shows itself as anger, isolation, lying, denial, minimizing, rationalizing and blaming—anything that will divert the focus away from the addict and his behaviors.

Your husband's survival personality may have said things like:

- You just don't turn me on anymore
- You've gotten fat
- I need more sex than you can give me
- If you satisfied me more, I wouldn't need to do this
- This is just how I am and you need to accept it
- I have some unusual sex needs and I don't think you'd be willing to meet them
- I'm just not interested in sex with you
- I have an especially low (or high) sex drive
- You're just overreacting. Everybody does it

On one level, the addict may even be able to convince themselves that these are, indeed, the reasons behind their actions. Such rationalizations enable the sex addict to numb some of his or her own guilt and shame.

It can not be said often enough—your husband's actions and attitudes are NOT YOUR FAULT! Even if there is a measure of truth in his statements (ie: you have gained weight or you refuse to participate in certain sexual activity), this does not give him license to break your wedding vows.

A man that doesn't have compulsions he believes he must protect is usually more willing to discuss, compromise, and resolve any issues that are hurting his marriage instead of using them as excuses for his behavior.

Q When I try to confide in my friend she says things like "boys will be boys", "men are more sexual" and "men need variety—they get bored." Is what she says true?

A It is true that each gender's approach to sexuality is very different. It is widely acknowledged that men are very visual creatures. They are significantly attracted, and affected sexually, by what they see. But God didn't just leave men out on a limb destined to a life of lust and sin. In His commitment to completeness, He also instilled a deep longing in the heart of women to be seen and desired.

In the context of an ideal world, this dynamic works perfectly. The natural yearning of a woman to be desirable attracts the attention of a man. His visual drivenness spurs him to pursue her and in the ensuing monogamous relationship that God intended, the play between the desirer and the desired works together to build a strong, unbreakable union.

God instilled these intense desires in us to serve two purposes. The first is to insure the continuance of the human race through procreation; the other is to bind husband and wife together. Studies have shown that when a person is involved sexually with another person, neurochemical changes occur in both their brains that encourage limbic, emotional bonding. In Christian settings we call this the "one flesh union."

Unfortunately, since these natural drives are so intense, the enemy sees them as the perfect vehicle to bring about pain and confusion. Any time he successfully tempts us with sexual activity outside the marriage, we bond with that person and, in effect, splinter off a piece of ourselves. Brain scanning has shown that even orgasming while using pornography or fantasy, effects the activity in our brains and bonds us to those images by searing them into our memory.

Centuries of sinful sexual behavior have created a society that no longer understands these natural tendencies as a way to bond with our mates. We have turned them outward. Men use their visual natures as an excuse to lust; women become more proactive to fill their yearning to be desired. Sex has become a distorted way to self gratify and feel valuable. Since uncommitted sex never satisfies, we've gotten increasingly desperate in our sexual pursuits. Popular beliefs are merely attempts to rationalize and excuse the emptiness we experience outside of God's plan.

Q I feel horrible, I know he has a problem. But I get so frustrated and angry sometimes. It seems like it's always all about tiptoeing around him. What about my needs?

A One of the biggest frustrations of being married to an addict is the fact that his needs often seem to overshadow those of everyone around him. Addiction, by its very nature causes an individual to become very self-focused. At times they can seem almost blind to the needs of others.

Finding a healthy balance in dealing with the injustice of his needs versus yours can be extremely challenging. If you are too "understanding" he may get the feeling that he has license to stay where he is. Conversely, being too demanding can cause him to feel threatened and send him deeper into his addiction. Where the line is drawn is usually best determined by his heart direction.

If your husband is still actively pursuing his addiction it is important to allow him to feel the full consequences of his actions. Don't make it too easy for him; don't cover-up for him; don't just "accept it." You can't allow yourself to continue to die inside. If you deny that your spouse has a problem or try to ignore its seriousness, you will do great damage to yourself, your husband, and the other people that rely on him.

If, however, your spouse has acknowledged his problem and his need for help and is attempting to move toward healing, you may decide it is beneficial to temporarily put some of your needs on the back burner for the long term good of your marriage. During the early stages of his recovery there can be a fine line between challenging him and abusing him by trying to push him too fast. Allowing him to heal at the speed that he can handle will likely require significant patience and sacrifice from you.

It is important that you surround yourself with a community of other women that understand what you are going through to pray with you and support you through the hard decisions that you will be forced to make. It is often very difficult to see clearly in the midst of the pain and emotion of the situation.

You need people that will:

- listen
- allow you to vent anger and frustration
- validate your pain
- remind you that this is not your fault
- not attempt to "fix" you
- help you see distorted thinking and lies
- flesh out Jesus' love to you consistently and faithfully

The shame and embarrassment you may feel about your situation can make it a challenge to reach out to others. Most of us fear that people will look down on us or reject us when we tell them what's going on—and, unfortunately, some may. If you run into one of them, don't give up. There are *many* others out there who will *gladly* provide the support and encouragement that each one of us needs and deserves at times like this.

Q This isn't the first time. He keeps promising that he'll never do it again, but then he does. I truly meant my marriage vows, but how long do I have to put up with this?

A As shown in the Cycle of Addiction (page 39), after the acting out part of the cycle has been completed and normalization has been achieved, the cognitive brain kicks in again. It is at this point that the addict feels the shame of their actions and experiences intense guilt, despair and contempt for themselves and others. They very often make vows to themselves and their loved ones about never doing those things again. They honestly mean what they say, but later, when the limbic system is triggered again, the cognitive brain with all its resolutions will shut down in favor of the reactive limbic brain once more.

It's a little like having two gas tanks on a truck. When you switch to the second tank you no longer have access to the fuel in the first tank and vice versa. When your husband is in the "reacting" limbic mode his cognitive thinking is shut down. Unlike switching gas tanks though, the switch to the limbic "tank" is not a choice, it happens automatically every time the pain becomes too great or he feels his survival is threatened. He, at this point, cannot control which tank he is in. The cycle is doomed to continue . . . pain; reaction; thinking; shame . . .pain, reaction, thinking, shame . . . until the underlying feelings and beliefs that set the cycle in motion are addressed.

Once your husband begins to honestly look at the source of his pain and the automatic responses that are triggered, he can learn ways to circumvent that shutting down of the cognitive thinking. Even if they hate where they are, most men have some reticence about starting the recovery process. The idea of replacing lifelong beliefs and habits with something that is yet unknown is difficult and scary.

If, however, your husband consistently refuses to go for help it is unlikely that things will improve. When, and if, you should, at some point, give up on the relationship is a question only you and God can answer.

Healing for your husband and your marriage is always the ideal, but there may come a time when enough is enough. It is not, however, a decision to be made lightly. Diligently seeking your own healing and recovery will help you get closer to God and become more equipped to make the right decisions for everyone involved.

Q There's a part of me that is desperate to hear all the details about what he has done. As his wife, don't I have a right to know what he's been doing?

A Because of the addict's intense fear of rejection, it is rare that the initial disclosure is the whole story. It is important, therefore, to have the opportunity to ask questions and receive truthful answers. In fact, you won't be able to truly forgive your husband until:

1. **You have counted the cost**

   It is important that the two of you work toward being able to talk about what has happened and how it has affected you, your marriage and your family on the deepest level. You can't move on until you fully understand and come to terms with the total extent of your losses.

2. **You believe he "gets" how deeply you have been violated**

   Don't be afraid to share your grief and pain with your husband and let him experience some of the turmoil you are going through. It is not unusual, however, for an addict to appear insensitive to a spouse's anger and hurt by expressing a desire for them to hurry up and get over their reaction to his betrayal. Your husband's impatience is most likely rooted in his lifelong effort to avoid feeling pain. Realizing that he caused such devastation is often difficult for him to bear.

   It is important for your own healing, however, to allow yourself to be where you are and not where you or anyone else thinks you *should* be.

3. You've had the chance to ask questions

Although it is important for you to know the facts about your husband's activities, be cautious about how many details you ask for. You will have to live with the information you receive. Women often express regret over having insisted on hearing the specific details of what happened. They say that it is very difficult to get those images out of their minds and that these thoughts can actually get in the way of healing and reconciliation. Examine why you need to know these things. Keep in mind that the only point of bringing up the past is to look for solutions for the future.

Q I can't stand his constant lying. Will it ever stop?

A Lying is a universal issue in all addictions. Addicts lie because, as strange as it may seem, they have grown to rely on the addiction to cope with life. When they stumbled upon this "answer" that distracts, calms and normalizes, they stopped seeking or learning other healthier ways to cope with the normal stresses and situations of life. Feeling that they know no other way to deal with fear, rejection, anxiety, boredom, and other de-stabilizers, their addictive behaviors take on a life and death importance. As much as the addict may hate being controlled by the addiction, deep down they are afraid that they won't be able to survive without it. They are lying to protect the only way they know how to handle life.

As hard as their lies are to live with, it is important that you don't take them personally. Your husband is not intentionally trying to hurt you. His lying started long ago, when he first refused to acknowledge to himself that he had a problem, and quickly spread to an ever-widening circle of people as his addiction progressed.

Of all addictions, sexual addiction seems to carry the greatest stigma and shame which gives strugglers even more reasons to lie:

- They lie because they feel ashamed or embarrassed.
- They lie to cover-up their involvement in sinful behaviors.
- They lie to avoid confrontations they have no tools to handle.
- They lie to escape criticism, blame, or feared rejection.
- They lie to avoid having to make changes that terrorize them.
- They lie because they have learned from past experience that they can get away with it with very minimal consequences.

These men can often be extremely honest in other areas of their lives, but will consistently default to lying whenever they feel the need to protect their addiction or avoid anticipated rejection.

Having to admit the depth of their struggle; fully accepting the blame for letting it continue; and acknowledging the intensity of the pain they have caused their loved ones, would be almost more than the addict could bear. To avoid it altogether, lying—even to themselves—becomes second nature.

The lies are likely to lessen as your husband finds healing, but because they have become an automatic habit, it may take quite a length of time for them to stop altogether.

Tempering your reaction to any disclosures that he makes — large or small—will help retrain his subconscious brain that it is safe to risk telling the truth. Confessions are seldom perfect and complete at first, but little by little he will learn that, contrary to what he has believed, the truth actually brings him freedom.

Q **Wouldn't it be easier to divorce? Is all this pain and struggle worth it?**

A When a situation is very painful, everything in us cries out for relief. Whatever it takes, we just want the hurting to stop. It's not unusual for wives of addicts to sometimes wish that their husband would have a heart attack or get hit by a truck. It's not because they are evil women—they just want something to happen that will make the horrible, awful pain and shame go away.

Other women start looking at divorce as a way to relieve the pain. Unfortunately, divorce is never the easy answer we've hoped for. It may put a little distance between you and the problem, but it doesn't solve a thing. He'll still be addicted, you'll still be wounded and your children will be deeply affected by *both* the divorce and the ongoing addiction. No one "wins" in a divorce.

Many women we have worked with have wrestled with questions like "Why am I still with him?" "What's the matter with me that I don't just up and leave? Don't I have any self respect?" They don't realize that it may be because God hasn't put it on their heart to go. His work in their lives and marriage may not be finished.

If we diligently seek God through this difficult time, he *will* direct our path. He is the only one who truly knows your husband's heart. He will make it clear to you whether you should go or stay.

I have seen several instances where wives who had been faithfully trying, forgiving, and encouraging their unrepentant spouses for years, came to a place where they felt God was telling them "It is finished. You have done all I asked, and I release you from your marriage." They ultimately did end their marriage, but it wasn't out of anger or retaliation, it was with a sad heart and a clear directive from God. God has since blessed these women abundantly.

Still others have *not* received that release, even though their husbands' continued failures, negative attitudes, and lack of motivation for recovery made their situations look completely hopeless. In these cases, God knew something that these women didn't know.

Even though their friends thought they were insane, each of them stuck with it in spite of the dismal circumstances. They didn't stay because they were afraid of a future alone, or because they were codependent. They stayed because they believed God told them to stay and, in time, they greatly rewarded for their patience. Their husbands *did* turn around and their marriages are better today than any of them ever dreamed they could be.

One woman had a husband that repeatedly sought relationships outside their marriage. He was angry and never accepted any fault for straying or hurting his family. His wife shared that in their entire marriage he had never apologized for *anything*. Their history had convinced her that he would never be able to take responsibility, or even acknowledge the pain he had caused. It seemed hopeless.

When she asked "How long do I need to put up with this?" we suggested that she seek God for an answer to that very important question. The very next week she came back with her answer. God had directed her to a story in Luke 13:6:

> *"Then he told this parable: A man had a fig tree, planted in his vineyard and he went to look for fruit on it, but did not find any. So he said to the man who took care of the vineyard, 'For three years now, I've been coming to look for fruit on this fig tree and haven't found any. Cut it down! Why should it use up the soil?'*
> *'Sir,' the man replied, 'leave it alone for one more year, and I'll dig around it and fertilize it. If it bears fruit next year, fine! If not, then cut it down.'"*

God was asking *her* to wait for one more year, as he worked on their behalf. Long before that year was up, things began to change. In just a few months she actually heard her husband speak those words of apology that she was so sure she would never hear. God knew that there was hope for that marriage in spite of the outward signs and he held her feet there until it could be revealed.

No one but God can tell *you* the right thing to do. Seek him and he will direct your path in the way that is best for everyone.

Q **I feel so much shame about my husband's behaviors . . . how can I ever get past it?**

A Shame is a common human reaction when we feel we have failed to meet society's expectations or our own personal standards of behavior and achievement.

Your husband's disclosure may well have set off a torrent of internal talk that included some of these common false beliefs:

- "It's all my fault"
- "If anyone knew about this, they wouldn't like me"
- "I'm trapped. There's nothing I can do to change the situation."
- "I'm less than or different than other people. I don't fit in."
- "I'm stupid (or naive) for not seeing this sooner."
- "I always get the short end of the stick"

If we accept these lies as true, they will inevitably take control of our entire self image. We will become convinced that we are bad or flawed, and that those faults are a permanent condition. The resulting shame leads to an overwhelming sense of powerlessness that destroys both our confidence and self-worth. We begin to believe that our life is ruined and that we are unlovable. Ironically, we usually react to these beliefs with blaming, anger and other limbic responses that *do* push people away and leave us isolated and alone.

The steps for reversing this devastating spiral are outlined on the following page. As the chart illustrates, the real secret to reducing shame is honesty with yourself and others, vulnerability, risking, and finding and nurturing relationships with safe, non-judgmental people. In a nutshell, to live without shame we must choose authenticity. Unless we begin to talk about the fears, shame and other feelings that get in the way of us living in freedom, we will find it virtually impossible to fully accept or experience true love and joy.

Finding Freedom from Shame

ANALYZE the SITUATION

1. Step back from the shame-causing problem and view it in a different light — reframe it.
2. Look at the external factors that contributed to the situation.
3. Differentiate between what WE caused and what THEY caused. If THEI- choices created the problem and WE feel guilt and shame about it, it is FALSE guilt.
4. If your shame is because of something YOU did, acknowledge the difference between BEING a bad person and DOING something bad.

RESPOND APPROPRIATELY

IF **YOUR** ACTIONS CAUSED YOUR SHAME:

- Ask forgiveness for your sin or mistakes
- Take authority over the enemy & connected spirits
- Ask the Holy Spirit to free you from the shame

IF **THEIR** ACTIONS CAUSED YOUR SHAME:

- Confess to God that you're wrestling with shame
- Repent of all unforgiveness/ resentment toward offender
- Make a choice to forgive those who offended you & brought shame into your life

REACH OUT

DON'T BELIEVE EVERYTHING YOU THINK!
- Challenge shame-based thoughts and ask God to replace them with truth.

MAKE CONNECTIONS
- with family
- with friends
- with humanity
- with God.

Connecting with others helps increase self-acceptance which, in turn, helps us have more acceptance for others and allows us to realize:

"This is human
I am human
Others are human"

But What About. . .

Teach me knowledge and good judgment,
for I trust your commands .

- Psalm 119:66

I was married to a sex addict, but we didn't make it. I'm single now. How can I avoid this next time?

A

The best way to avoid getting involved with another sex addict is to work diligently on your own issues. Brokenness seems to attract brokenness. The healthier we are, the healthier people we will attract and the easier it will be to see the truth about them.

You are particularly vulnerable if:

- you appear too needy or demonstrate codependent tendencies
- you are afraid to be honest and ask honest questions
- you'll live with "unreasonable rules" just to have a man in your life.
- you are sexually broken or addicted yourself
- you think you can be the one to "free" them from their struggles.

He may struggle with sexual addiction if any of these red flags exist:

- he seems surrounded with secrecy/ has many "off limit" topics
- he is over-judgmental about how women dress/look/act
- he verbally sexualizes women in your presence
- he is over- (or under-) fixated with sexual things
- he seems asexual & has little interest in physical contact
- he is over-complimentary or uses lots of sexual innuendos

- he has excesses in other areas of his life (may indicate possible co-addictions)
- he seems stuck at the sexual/relational maturity of a teenager
- he doesn't seem fully present (robot-like) during sexual play
- he has a hard time getting emotionally close
- he has a history of extramarital affairs
- he finds non-relational sex intriguing (S&M, swinging, voyeurism)
- his money disappears quickly without an increase in tangible assets
- he insists on total financial control or won't let anyone see his bills
- he needs large amounts of "no questions allowed" private time
- women in his life seem relegated to a one-down position
- he attempts to spiritualize his inappropriate activities and attitudes
- he has a general aura of anger, agitation or self-hatred

If you see any of these signs, don't panic. There may be another explanation for these behaviors, but do proceed with caution and your eyes wide open. As you already know, a relationship with an unrecovering addict is lonely, belittling, and potentially damaging to your self-esteem and physical health.

Q Our problem is different—we don't have sex. It doesn't feel right, but I guess we can eliminate sexual addiction as the root cause since there is no sex . . . right?

A Wrong. Consider the fact that there are two main types of inappropriate relationships with food: one is bulimia (overeating/purging); the other is anorexia (not eating). Both ends of the spectrum are equally unhealthy and both will ultimately destroy the body.

The same is true for sex addicts. Both acting out and totally avoiding sex are equally devastating to the healthy intimacy that God intended. Many addicts (especially in the Christian community) totally shut down their sexuality in an attempt to end their acting out. In every sense of the word, they become asexual. This tactic can, for a time, be an effective way to curb the temptation to participate in inappropriate sexual behaviors—but, unfortunately, it is an all or nothing situation. If you shut off "bad sexuality", you shut off "good sexuality" as well.

Sexual anorexia is not the cure for sexual addiction. Many men mistakenly believe that since they are no longer acting out in the old way, they no longer have a problem. Their wives, however, are forced to live in a marriage devoid of sexual intimacy. There are a staggering number of marriages in our country in which sex is non-existent or, at best, highly infrequent for ten, twenty, thirty years or more. Even the church often sees this as a victory, because they are no longer participating in immoral or "sinful" activities.

The problem is that, even though they aren't acting out, the lack of normal sex indicates that they have not dealt with the underlying causes of their addiction. The pendulum has just swung to the other extreme.

Remember, the goal is much greater than just getting your husband to stop his behavior. The only real freedom comes when he willingly faces his pain and fears and accepts God as the source of true fulfillment and healing. The goal, therefore, is not control, but healthy sexuality and increased intimacy as a couple.

Q I have been told that I am being codependent about my husband's behaviors. What exactly does that mean?

A Unless they are in recovery, almost all spouses of addicts are codependent. There is something about the very nature of addiction that turns those around it into victims of the disease. Those with tender hearts and deep unmet needs are the most vulnerable.

It is very easy for a person who loves an addict to become so consumed with their spouse's problems that they don't have time to take care of themselves. Codependents appear to be depended upon, but they are dependent. They look strong, but feel helpless. They determine their self-worth by how well those around them are doing.

Common characteristics of a Codependent:

1. They struggle with balance in their lives. They are often overcommitted, yet have trouble saying "no."
2. They have difficulty identifying what they are feeling.
3. They take care of everyone but themselves.
4. They constantly feel like they're not measuring up which results in low self-esteem.
5. They attempt to control the thoughts, feelings, and actions of others.
6. They feel compelled to help other people solve their problems whether they want help or not.

7. They are willing to compromise their own values to avoid rejection.
8. They may use sex to gain approval or to keep a relationship.
9. They can appear controlling and manipulative.
10. They assign themselves the job of anticipating other people's needs.
11. They feel guilty if someone gives to them or treats them with respect.

To truly experience a healthy relationship, the codependent needs God's healing as much as the addict. Just like the addict, they need to acknowledge their fears and let God establish their value instead of having to "earn" it by being everybody's everything.

Q Why am I acting this way? Am I going crazy?

A In the midst of particularly traumatic times we often find ourselves acting in ways that seem out of character. If you are feeling suicidal or doing things that are illegal or could be dangerous to yourself or others, it is highly recommended that you seek a mental health evaluation, just to put your mind at ease.

In most cases, however, the underlying issue is not mental illness, but survival. The same limbic "survival" part of the brain that creates cravings for addictive behaviors when your husband is feeling stressed, fearful, or isolated is active in your life as well.

If life feels unsafe, the limbic part of your brain responds in one of these three ways to help you feel more secure and in control:

FIGHT (using ***anger*** to protect ourselves)

May look like:

- Explosive anger or actual fighting
- Sarcasm, gossiping or backbiting
- Being right, arguing, or blaming
- Workaholism
- Perfectionism
- People-pleasing

The more passive approaches of fighting are often overlooked, but are just as effective at gaining control of the situation or keeping the perceived danger at arms length.

FLIGHT (using ***avoidance*** to protect ourselves)

May look like:

- Physically running away
- Isolating
- Mindless activities
- Dangerous compulsions or addictions
- "Acceptable" compulsions or addictions

These behaviors help us escape from anything our brain tags as dangerous to our emotional or physical safety.

FREEZE (***shutting down*** to protect ourselves)

May look like:

- Getting sick
- Emotional numbing
- Minimizing
- Giving up / Learned Helplessness / Being a Victim
- Not trying unless certain of success
- Depression

These behaviors keep us from having to feel or deal with the situation

These automatic responses may be more intense or take a different form than the way you would normally react. Since limbic responses are not just about what is going on right now, but also incorporate pent-up feelings from similar past situations that are still unresolved, they often come across as extreme overreactions.

As we find healing for our wounds and resolve old issues, we will be more able to manage and take control of current situations in healthy ways instead of relying on these limbic reactions to cope.

Although, not a true limbic reaction, either fear or a lack of education about sexual addiction can create yet another source of unusual behavior. In an attempt to gain control over our husband's addictive behaviors that threaten our marriage and our family's future, we may take on unhealthy roles and behaviors of our own.

UNHEALTHY ROLES (leave us ***feeling empty***)

Detective - The compulsive need or desire to monitor your husband's actions.

Warden - Trying to control the addict and his behaviors.

Caretaker/Educator - Taking responsibility for his recovery.

Sex Toy - Trying to be or act out his fantasies

Accomplice - Covering up for him, making excuses and keeping his secrets.

Punisher - Taking on the job of making him pay for his sins.

Since none of these reflect God's intention for us as a wife, they will leave us frustrated, empty and feeling crazy. It is only with God's help and healing that we can make decisions and set boundaries that will be helpful to both us and our spouse.

Q **Why does everyone say I need to work on MY stuff? What stuff?**

A At first it doesn't make sense. What could *you* possibly need to work on? The whole situation is so far beyond your control. You can certainly attempt to push your husband into recovery. You can get angry. You can try be an encouragement. You can give ultimatums. But, deep down you know that unless *your husband* decides to seek help, there is nothing you can do to fix this.

Many women have admitted that discovering their husband's secret activities was one of the most traumatic events of their entire life. They were ill-prepared for the financial, emotional and social consequences the disclosure brought to the entire family—but, most especially to them, as the spouse.

It might help to compare your husband's addiction to being in a serious car accident. He was in the driver's seat. He made the choices. He's the one that either didn't see or didn't heed the oncoming danger. The crash was, most certainly, his fault. But, it really doesn't matter who was driving—you were *both* in the car, you *both* got hurt and you will *both* require emergency care.

Some of the wounds you sustained can be directly attributed to the accident: broken trust, self-doubt, shame, and any number of other conditions. But a collision can also reactivate wounds that you thought were healed long ago. This new betrayal may knock off old scabs and bring back vivid recollections of times in your past that others have betrayed and hurt you deeply. Old feelings of inadequacy, vulnerability, or hopelessness may also be reawakened.

The sheer magnitude of this trauma assault can often lead to significant health complications, both physically and mentally. You may notice an increase in physical illness, self-esteem issues, depression, or "getting even" behaviors. You may even feel like you are going to explode from the pressure of ping-ponging between experiencing intense hurt and embarrassment about what is going on and worrying that somehow you are responsible for your husband's problem or should have, at least, been able to see and stop it sooner.

You will likely need to find knowledgeable people to help you:

1. assess the damage that was done to you
2. work through the emotional pain, hurt feelings or anger that your husband's actions have caused
3. gain a clear understanding of sexual addiction
4. set appropriate boundaries with the addict and learn to be supportive without caretaking, enabling or controlling
5. develop new problem solving skills that will help you rebuild your self-esteem and self-confidence and reduce the emotional baggage that sabotages healthy relationships
6. determine what you are and are not willing to live with should there be a future relapse

Even if you can't see it right now, you *do* have significant power and control over your own life. You can recover from this, whether he chooses to or not. If the worst happens, and he never gets help, you will be empowered to make decisions for you and your children based on strength, not fear.

If your husband *does* decide to seek healing, there will be a whole other set of issues to work on. As he begins to understand himself and make the changes necessary to move toward freedom, it will change the dynamic between you. Much of it will be good, but the two of you may need help learning how to communicate and interact in a healthier, more satisfying way.

Q **I think I may be the one with the problem. Are women ever sex addicts?**

A It is estimated that 15-20% of women who are married to sex addicts struggle with sexual addiction themselves. In women it may show itself as an addiction to relationships, romance, fantasy, pornography/cybersex, masturbation or exhibitionism; or in selling/trading sex, partnering with another addict, binge and purge sexual activity or sexual anorexia.

Interestingly enough, a woman doesn't even have to enjoy the sexual experience to be addicted. Many women learn to tolerate sex to get what they really want—love, touch, nurture, assurance that they are OK or medication from emotional pain.

Women's Self-Test for Sexual Addiction

1. Do you believe your sexual behaviors are a problem?
2. Have you experienced negative consequences because of your sexual activities?
3. Do you repeatedly promise yourself or others that you will stop certain sexual behaviors, only to break those promises later?
4. Do you think you use sex to relieve anxiety or to escape from or cope with life?
5. Are you often preoccupied with sexual thoughts or romantic daydreams?
6. Do you ever feel guilty, depressed, or angry with yourself after sex?
7. Do you regularly purchase romance novels or sexually explicit books or magazines, rent X-rated movies, view internet pornography or visit online chat rooms?
8. Do you worry about people finding out about your sexual activities?

9. Do any of your sexual behaviors go against your values or beliefs and yet you continue to pursue them?
10. Do friends or family members ever voice worry or complaints about your sexual behavior?
11. Do you minimize, justify or lie to your family and friends about your sexual behavior?
12. Are you ever anxious for obligations or events with friends or family to end, so you can have time to pursue sexual activities?
13. Does the pursuit of sex cause you to be careless about yourself or the welfare of your family or others?
14. Do you regularly cruise the local "hot spots" in search of sexual encounters?
15. Have you ever had a sexual encounter with someone you met online via social media or adult chat rooms?
16. Have you ever participated in sexual activity in exchange for money, gifts or other services?
17. Do you often lose track of time while pursuing sexual activities?
18. Does your sexual behavior ever interfere with relations with your spouse or boyfriend?
19. As an adult, have you ever been sexual with someone under the age of 18?
20. Were you sexually abused as a child or adolescent?

Although far from a definitive diagnosis, if you answered "yes" to even a few of the first 19 questions, it is likely that you may be sexually addicted and could benefit from a deeper look into the issue.

What Now?

Show me your ways, Lord,
teach me your paths.

- Psalm 25:4

Q I love my husband. What can I do to help him find healing?

A

1. Work on your own stuff

A marriage is like a set of gears. Changing the shape of one of the gears will change the way they function together. By dealing with your own fears, self-doubts and codependency you will change the way you feel and react, which will subsequently change the face of your marriage.

2. Consider Intervention

If our loved one was sick and getting progressively worse, most of us would try to get him to see a doctor. If he continued to resist we might even schedule an appointment for him ourselves and insist on driving him to it. Very few of us would just stand by and watch our husband die without taking some kind of action. Sexual addiction is no less destructive than a debilitating disease. It may seem "victimless", but it will, in time, take the life of your spouse—spiritually, emotionally and often even physically.

Change is scary, especially when it involves our core survival tools. To entertain the idea of changing, the pain of where we are must become greater than the pain of leaving the familiar and moving toward something unknown. Intervention is a way of creating a crisis in the addict's life before they hit bottom and their life is totally destroyed. It *forces* them to choose which pain they prefer. It is a loving act that's intended solely to restore life to them.

3. Create a safer place

Recovery will be the hardest thing your husband has ever attempted. He needs an environment that is as safe as possible to test out new responses, learn to trust, and risk intimacy. Education about what he is going through along with your own recovery efforts will help make your home a safer place for healing.

4. Take care of yourself

At the beginning of every airline flight, the flight attendants present safety instructions. In the case of an emergency they always remind adults flying with small children or vulnerable adults to put the oxygen mask on *themselves* before they try assisting their loved ones. If they fail to do this and pass out from a lack of oxygen, they certainly won't be able to help anyone else.

If you truly want to be able to support and encourage your husband, you first need to make sure you're in as good a space as possible. Work to reduce outside stress, get plenty of rest and develop a support network of your own.

Memorizing the following truths will help you stay focused and less likely to accept emotional burdens that are not yours to carry:

The Five Realities of Your Situation

1. Your husband's struggle is ***not*** your fault.
2. This ***is*** a big deal.
3. Facing the ***truth*** is the way to ***freedom***.
4. You've been wounded and ***need healing***, too
5. You ***can't*** do this alone.

Q Is intervention Biblical?

A *Matthew 18:15-17 says "If your brother sins against you, go and show him his fault, just between the two of you. If he listens to you, you have won your brother over. But if he will not listen, take one or two others along, so that every matter may be established by the testimony of two or three witnesses. If he refuses to listen to them, tell it to the church; and if he refuses to listen even to the church, treat him as you would a pagan or tax collector."*

For some reason, we have traditionally exempted the marriage relationship from this process. We have erroneously believed that when we uttered "til death do us part" we lost the right to comment about our spouses actions—even when they are putting themselves (and sometimes us) in jeopardy. The Bible tells us that if we see a brother (and that includes our husband) living in sin and distorted thinking, it is our obligation to try to restore him to truth.

Intervention should not be done without extensive planning. Although the scriptural "first step" is to confront your spouse on a one-to-one basis, you may decide it is wiser to move directly to a group intervention. Addicts are skilled at denial and delusion. You shouldn't even consider confronting your spouse alone unless you can honestly and confidently answer yes to the following questions:

1. **Can you confront the addict with a spirit of love and gentleness?**

2. **Are you strong enough to withstand your spouse's disapproval?**

3. **Can you follow through and stick to what you say you will do?**

4. **Are you absolutely sure that confronting your spouse will not put you in any physical danger?**

Once you have determined the best way to proceed, all who will be participating need to understand the objectives of the intervention.

Intervention is ***not*** **treatment.** It is getting them to get help.

Intervention is ***not*** **placing blame.** It is affirming the person's value to you, in spite of their imperfections and behaviors.

Intervention is ***not*** **resolving hurt.** It is acknowledging the impact the person's behaviors have had on you.

Intervention is ***not*** **demanding change.** It is offering to help someone begin to regain control over their life.

Intervention is ***not*** **begging, pleading or bargaining.** It is affirming your love, setting limits and offering professional help.

Intervention is ***not*** **threatening.** It is refusing to help someone continue hurting themselves and allowing them to experience the natural consequences of their choices.

Intervention is ***not*** **manipulating or coercing.** It is helping them decide they need help.

Above all else, it is important to remember that Biblical intervention is not about punishment or control—it is about restoration.

"If someone is caught in sin, you who are spiritual should restore him gently." Galatians 6:1

How does intervention work? Tell me more about the process.

Intervention involves confronting the addict with a spirit of love and gentleness. It usually follows this basic form:

1. **Confront the behaviors you know about.**
   "I care about you, but I am concerned about some of your behaviors. By those I mean. . . (list the known FACTS of their sexual acting out.)"

2. **Share YOUR experience with getting help.**
   Describe your own addictive behaviors, fears, and your process of getting help. If you can't relate personally to addiction, share the story of someone you know that got help (don't use names.)

3. **Try to empathize with the sex addict.**
   "It must be lonely. You must be tired and frightened." Talk only of feelings. Avoid diagnosing the problem and judgmental comments.

4. **Tell them how their behavior has affected you.**
   "When you did . . . (list behavior) it really hurt me and I got really angry" or "that really embarrassed or caused me harm" (describe the harm done only to YOU. Do not talk about harms to others.)

5. **State the behavioral changes you desire.**
   "Please do not touch me in that way. Please do not ask me for . . . (describe the sexual behavior.) I expect you to be sexually faithful."

6. **Describe the consequences of noncompliance.**
   "If you do these things again, this is what I will do (describe)."

7. **State clearly where help is available.**
   Have phone numbers, meeting information, etc. ready.

8. **Restate your love and concern for the addict.**
   "I care for you. I value our relationship and want to see it continue. I hope and pray that you can get some help for yourself."

Adapted from the book *Faithful & True* by Mark Laaser, Ph.D

Q What if he gets angry and refuses to do anything about his problem?

A Interventions can be highly emotional. There may be blame, tears, or out and out denial of the claims that have been made. The addict may even act like an offended victim, shocked and distraught over the "unfairness" of their loved one's words.

You must be prepared for the possibility that he won't listen to what you have to say, won't accept the help that is being offered and may even become angry with you. If this happens you need to realize that their anger and defensiveness has nothing to do with what you have done, how you have done it, or you as a person. It is more likely that they feel that their very survival is in jeopardy.

Since acting out has been the means by which the addict has been able to avoid pain and fear, they may subconsciously feel that this survival mechanism must be preserved, at all cost. They can't imagine functioning without it. The strange juxtaposition of hating what it is doing to their life and yet, at the same time, protecting it above all else shows just how strong the grip of addiction can be.

If your husband does not respond to the initial intervention, you may need to enlist the help of additional people to support you in your efforts. Sex addicts who are denying that they have a problem need to hear evidence that provides proof of their current condition. They need to know that more than one person has seen and felt the consequences of their behavior.

If you go through the entire Biblical process of intervention and your husband still refuses to get help, you have no choice but to proceed with the consequences you discussed during the intervention. Any softening at this point may lead him to believe that he has, once again, maneuvered his way out of trouble.

If he finds that, in time, you will back down and he can safely continue his behavior without fear of long-term consequences, your words become hollow and any future efforts on your behalf to try to move him toward recovery will have little impact.

It can be very difficult to watch someone you love have to suffer the consequences of their choices, but it's important to remember that in his addiction he is on the road to spiritual, emotional and maybe even physical death. He may be angry with you for a time, but as he begins to heal, it is likely that he will realize that your actions were borne out of love.

Q I feel like I'm going to burst. How can I find a safe place to talk to about this?

A INDIVIDUAL OR COUPLE COUNSELING

A counselor can be very helpful *if* they understand addiction. Unfortunately, many counselors have not had experience in this arena and can create a very unsafe environment for addicts and their spouses. Asking these five questions of a potential counselor can help you find a therapist that will have the skills and understanding that you need:

1. **Do you acknowledge sexual addiction as a real and treatable addictive problem?**

   Unenlightened counselors may view sexual addiction as simply bad behavior, a sin problem, or a "boys will be boys" lust problem. All of these are an oversimplification of a difficult multifaceted problem. Behavioral change, repentance, or squelching of the lustful nature are not sufficient to bring about a permanent change.

2. **Have you had experience successfully treating sexual addiction?**

   Many counselors, especially in the secular community, have had little or no success in their attempts help those struggling with sexual addiction. It is important to find an individual who has a solid history of working with these types of compulsive behaviors and a notable track record of long term relapse prevention in their clients.

3. **What do you believe are the core issues of sexual addiction?**

   Popular therapy often cites lust as the core issue of sexual addiction. The Christian community may deal with it as a sin issue. Although both lust and sin are involved, they are only symptoms of the fear and trauma that are the real core issues of sexual addiction.

4. **What, if any, Christian beliefs, activities, or resources do you utilize in your treatment approach?**

   The most promising therapy processes for sexual addiction rely heavily on the Holy Spirit and prayer to isolate core beliefs, and help renounce survival lies that have been accepted as truth.

5. **What, in your opinion, can a wife do to help a husband that is struggling with sexual issues?**

   If there is any indication that a counselor believes that the wife is overreacting to her husband's actions or that they think that sexier underwear, increased sexual initiation, or a more open mind on the part of the wife will solve the problem, this is not a person that can help.

PROCESSING GROUPS

If available in your area, you might also benefit from participating in a support group or group therapy. Studies have shown that being with other people that understand your struggle, without having to explain it, creates chemical changes in your brain that contribute to well-being and happiness.

The opportunity to work on issues and talk with others that are going through exactly what you are going through can greatly accelerate the recovery process for both the addict and the spouse.

Not only is it hugely beneficial to realize that you're not alone in your situation, but increased feedback, seeing how others handle similar problems, and the support and encouragement of peers provides us with new understanding and helps us take the risks required to make positive changes in our lives.

Q How can I ever respect him again?

A Ephesians 5 commands us to respect our husbands:

"However each one of you also must love his wife as he loves himself, ***and the wife must respect her husband.****"—Ephesians 5:33.*

We've probably all heard sermons and marriage seminars on this passage, but how in the world can we still be held to this standard when our husband is involved in such unrespectable behaviors, and we feel anything but loved?

Although it may *seem* that we shouldn't be required to respect him if we don't feel like we're getting the love we're due, this passage is talking about an *unconditional* love and respect. Unconditional means "without conditions or limitations; absolute." It is not an "if, then" equation. It doesn't have to be earned. We give it freely because it is the right thing to do and what God asks of us. Of course, God's intention is that your husband would also *love* you unconditionally, but even in the absence of that, the instruction to respect our husbands still stands.

But how?

How can we respect someone who is caught in addiction and doing "those" totally unrespectable things? We certainly don't *feel* much respect for them.

If you look closer at the whole Ephesians 5 chapter, though, you'll find it isn't talking about feelings. It is talking about *cognitive* choices. Among other things, it mentions *imitating* in verse 1, *being careful* in verse 15, *submitting* in verse 22, and in verse 33—*loving* and *respecting*. Each one of them is an intentional choice, not a feeling.

The secret to obeying Ephesians 5:33 isn't just sitting around waiting for those respectful feelings to return. It is making a deliberate choice to show respect in obedience to God.

Remember reading about the limbic brain? That's where our feelings reside. And, since the limbic brain only learns from experience, it usually requires many, many positive repetitions to rewrite the brain and bring about those *feelings* of respect or love. The cognitive brain, that holds our morals, values, and reasoning power, is the part that allows us to *act* respectful or loving, based on intentional choices.

Basically we must continue to choose to be respectful until we've had enough positive experiences with this person that our limbic brain decides they are safe and worthy of our respect. That's when we actually start *feeling* respectful.

A similar dynamic will come into play once your husband has gained some healing and is truly trying to show sincere love for you. It will take time and many repetitions of kindness and protection for your limbic brain to be able to believe that your husband's new behavior is real, safe, and able to be trusted.

So, what does choosing to respect look like?

A man's heart longs to hear that others believe in him. That we think he has what it takes. That feels like respect to him.

But what if we're not sure that he *does* have what it takes? What if we're pretty sure he doesn't? What then?

God doesn't want us to be phony. It's not a fake it 'til you make it scenario. We must search our hearts for what we can truthfully affirm in our husbands.

Often it may only be something like "I believe that if you reach out to God and seek his direction, you can do this." Your trust is really more in God, and not your husband, at this point, but it is likely something you can say with truth and confidence that will let your husband know that you believe he can succeed.

Remember, we can always, with God's help, choose to *act* respectful. *Feeling* respectful will take time.

Q **After all we've been through, how can we ever rebuild the trust that was lost? Is it even possible?**

A Yes! Working together, the trust in your marriage can *absolutely* be restored—but you can't expect it to happen overnight. Just as it takes time to actually start *feeling* respect for your husband again, it will take time for your limbic brain to become fully convinced that he is truly committed to change; no longer a significant threat to your safety; and able to be counted on to care about, and meet, your basic emotional needs.

The first step is obviously his. Unless he chooses to seek help and healing with the guidance of a trained professional, it is unlikely that he will be able to maintain any lasting change in his attitude or behaviors. Once he has actually begun the recovery process in earnest, however, your participation becomes as essential as his in rebuilding your relationship.

When someone has hurt us deeply, our automatic reaction is to pull away. Subconsciously, we begin creating a wall between us to insure that they will never be able to hurt us like that again. To have any hope of re-establishing trust we must resist our natural inclination and cautiously begin dismantling this wall of self-protection.

A number of years ago, God showed me an important truth about my relationship with him, that I have come to realize is also true in our earthly relationships. At the time I was frustrated by the fact that even though God had always shown himself to be faithful in my life, I still found myself worrying about various situations—an indication that I was not trusting. I asked him in prayer how I could learn to trust him more. God very clearly told me that the more I got to know him, and his character, the more I would find myself trusting him. Trust wasn't something I had to muster up, it would be the natural outcome of truly getting to know him.

It is the unknown and the unpredictable that we are really afraid of. When we don't know what's in someone's heart and head we don't know what they are thinking or how they will react to a given situation. It's that not knowing that makes us feel unsafe.

As I get to know God in a deeper way, I am learning what to expect from him. More and more I can relax. I don't need to be so on guard or wonder what God is thinking about me. And, I *do* find myself increasingly able to trust him in many areas of my life.

Not knowing what your husband is thinking or doing or how he will react to certain situations will similarly diminish your ability to trust him, especially now. We need to turn *toward* them and get to know their heart, their beliefs and their fears so we can better understand what makes them tick and how they will respond to particular situations.

The challenge that often makes this a long process, is that most sex addicts have so much shame and so many distorted beliefs about themselves and others that it is not easy for them to allow people to get to know them in the deep way that encourages trust. Little by little the recovery process will help rewrite some of these old beliefs and help them risk sharing more of themselves. With God's help, you can provide a safe place for him to experiment with these new skills, as well as hone your own ability to share yourself.

As you both learn to communicate with a whole new level of transparency you will, simultaneously, be getting to know the true character of each other in a way you've never been able to before. One day, it will surprise you to realize just how much trust has been created as a natural outcome of your new deeper relationship.

Q Can you recommend any books that might help me deepen my understanding of sexual addiction?

A There are many books on the market about sexual addiction. Unfortunately, most of them focus on treating the symptoms of the struggle (such as lust or sin) and not the underlying causes. Others use shame as a means to facilitate behavioral change. Neither of these strategies are effective in bringing about permanent transformation. Only the healing power of Jesus and his gentle rewriting of our tightly held survival lies can restore our lives to what he originally intended. There are a few books that you may find helpful, however:

- **Breaking Free: Understanding Sexual Addiction & the Healing Power of Jesus** *by Russell Willingham*

  One of the best resources we've found. This very realistic, yet hopeful, book proclaims the forgiveness and healing that Jesus offers. Speaking out of his own experience and those that he has counseled, Willingham shares practical steps that can help people break the chains of this addiction.

- **Now Choose Life!: One Man's Journey Out of the Grip of Pornography** *by Janet K Wheeler with Recollections & Epilogue by Bruce Wheeler*

  This book provides poignant glimpses into Bruce's thirty-year battle with sexual addiction woven together with easy-to-understand professional commentary. It dispels many of the rampant myths and misconceptions about this little understood addiction and provides indispensable information, empowering hope and a proven way out of the grip of sexual sin for every struggler.

- **Surfing for God: Discovering the Divine Desire Beneath Sexual Struggle**
  by Michael John Cusick
  Another great resource. Cusick uses examples from his own life and his twenty years of counseling experience to help readers understand how porn struggles begin, how to prevent them, and most importantly how to overcome the compulsion once it begins. This is a powerful book full of truth and hope.

- **Out of the Shadows / Contrary to Love / Don't Call it Love / In the Shadow of the Net**
  all by Patrick Carnes, Ph.D
  Dr. Carnes is a pioneer in the study of sex addiction. Although not written from a Christian perspective, his books are still very helpful and highly informative.

- **No Stones**
  by Marnie Ferree
  As a recovering sex addict herself, Marnie has written one of the first books that specifically speaks hope to the many women who struggle with sexual addiction.

- **Faithful & True: Sexual Integrity in a Fallen World**
  by Mark Laaser, Ph.D.
  Dr. Laaser offers a comprehensive overview of sexual addiction, its roots, its consequences, and its treatment.

- **The Pornography Trap**
  by Ralph Earle & Mark Laaser
  Addresses the sexual sin epidemic that is sweeping through our churches infecting both church leaders and their congregations. Especially helpful for pastors, counselors and ministry leaders.

- **Steering Clear / Restoring the Fallen**
  both by Earl Wilson
  Earl shares his personal journey as well as his experiences as a counselor and teacher on the issues of addiction and restoration.

JOURNAL/DISCUSSION QUESTIONS

Many women have found journaling to be a helpful way of processing their feelings. These questions may help you get started.

1. **What insights come to mind as you reflect on the information in this booklet? How do they apply to your life?**

2. **What have you lost because of your husband's problem?**

3. In this situation, what are the things that you can control and what things are out of your control?

4. What was the biggest misconception you had before reading this material? How has your thinking changed?

5. What is your current biggest struggle or frustration?

6. What will you do next? What is your next step?

7. Who can you recruit to help you through this process?

We also invite you to read the Wheeler's personal story, written by Janet:

Now Choose Life!

One Man's Journey
Out of the Grip of Pornography

"Now Choose Life! *is a wonderful resource that will inform, inspire, motivate and remind every couple that there is hope ahead! Bruce shares raw details of his life journey out of the grip of sexual addiction. His story is inspiring, illustrating that there is hope for the sex addict even after divorce. Janet shares her insights about sex addiction and how devastating the behaviors are to addicts and those who love them. This book will help addicts, partners, families and the friends who love them."* —***Cory M. Schortzman**, Executive Director at Transformed Hearts Counseling Center in Colorado Springs, Colorado*

There is hope!

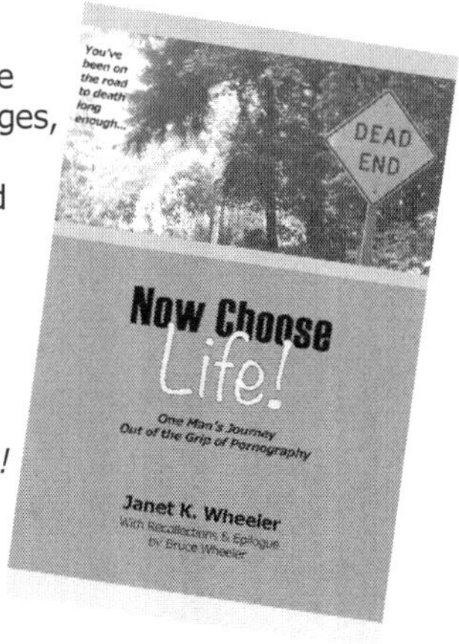

Pornography, affairs and other compulsive sexual behaviors are destroying the marriages, careers and self-respect of hundreds of thousands of upstanding citizens, dedicated Christians and all-around nice people. My husband was one of them.

Through poignant glimpses into his thirty-year battle with sexual addiction woven together with easy-to-understand professional commentary, *Now Choose Life!* dispels many of the rampant myths and misconceptions about this little understood addiction and provides indispensable information, empowering hope and a proven way out of the grip of sexual sin for every struggler.

Now Choose Life! is a down-to-earth account of how regular people like us, in all our brokenness and imperfection, found our way out of the private hell of sexual addiction. It illustrates, in very practical terms, the process of true recovery with all its ups and downs and shows how even the most tenuous Christian can learn to partner with God to find and heal the wounds that have created and fueled their addictive behaviors. It's a story of lasting victory and freedom—not just for us—but for *all* who choose to embark on the amazing journey to take back their lives from the enemy's grip.

Now Choose Life! will benefit *anyone* who seeks a deeper understanding of sexual addiction and the path to lasting freedom.

Opened My Eyes

This is a brutally honest book about how one man became embroiled in sexual addiction and fought hard to escape it. As the wife of a sexual addict, this book really opened my eyes to the absolute grip of the compulsion that a sexual addict faces. I guess I never fully realized the full force of this compulsion and how the addiction isn't really about sex; but rather about other things - such as escape, comfort, safety, etc. I also was able to see that a man can truly love his wife and have this addiction, because his wife is the one he loves, but the sexual desire he has for others is about sex. I have always had a hard time seeing this, but I understand so much more now. I would encourage anyone who is facing this kind of an addiction to read this book. It will help you understand more fully what is going on in the mind of the addict and help you process what has happened in your own situation. — K.

Courageous

"Now Choose Life! *is an insightful book that delves into a "forbidden" subject—sexual addiction and pornography. The damage they cause both the addict and those close to them is very real and painful. This book, written from the hearts of two courageous Christians, with God's guidance and love, will provide a deep knowledge and understanding that can, indeed, lead to new life." — Jane S.*

Insightful, heartbreaking, and hopeful!

This book is written in such a way that it is like listening to an orchestra rather than a single instrument. Often books like this are a one-person memoir. But this tells Bruce's story with memories from the time he was a toddler, with commentary by Janet as a wife and counselor, with the added layer of research and science to give the reader a clear understanding of this devastating addiction. I would recommend this book for anyone interested in understanding the causes of sexual addiction. Bruce and Janet Wheeler have bravely and compellingly cleared away the shadows and shown a path to healing. — L.M. Puhlman

Couldn't put it down

When I got the book I starting reading and found it hard to put down. Janet Wheeler did an excellent job of tying together Bruce's comments and a clinical appraisal to his problem. I finished the book in ONE DAY....By the time I finished I not only thought I knew both Bruce and Janet but also found myself wanting to meet these two exceptional people. I applaud their courage and perseverance and hope their book will be of help to others trying to beat this, or any addiction. Every church library should have a copy of this book on their shelves! — Dot. M.

A must read!

Bruce's testimony, along with his wife's interpretation of the reality of the disease of sexual addiction and how it affected them, can unlock doors for people who already know they have a problem and are seeking help. It will also answer a lot of questions for people that are reading about the subject of sexual addiction for the first time. It may even explain what they've been feeling, themselves. — Sherry M.

Now Choose Life!
is currently available in Paperback and Kindle Versions

More information
at www.lifemoreabundant.net

To Contact Janet

Janet Wheeler is affiliated with
Life More Abundant Network
Bellingham, Washington
360-223-1862

For more information about sexual addiction or Life More Abundant Network please visit our website:
www.lifemoreabundant.net

For daily encouragement we invite you to read our blog:
blog.lifemoreabundant.net

Contact Janet directly via e-mail:
janet@lifemoreabundant.net